DESEGREGATION
IN
Northern Virginia
LIBRARIES

DESEGREGATION
IN
Northern Virginia
LIBRARIES

CHRIS BARBUSCHAK & SUZANNE S. LAPIERRE

Foreword by Dr. Sujatha Hampton of the Fairfax County NAACP

THE
History
PRESS

Published by The History Press
Charleston, SC
www.historypress.com

First published 2023

Manufactured in the United States

ISBN 9781467152891

Library of Congress Control Number: 2022944984

This book is dedicated to those whose efforts to desegregate libraries in Virginia and elsewhere in America paved the way for more equitable library services for all.

CONTENTS

CONTENTS

FOREWORD

*I*n April 2021, I attended an information session about the Fairfax Library Foundation for new members of the Fairfax County Library Board of Trustees. Foundation staff shared an excellent presentation about their mission and scope of work, their budget priorities, their outreach and general information about how the library foundation and the Fairfax County Public Libraries (FCPL) work together to build, maintain and grow the outstanding library system our community has come to rely on.

At the time of that meeting, Fairfax County was grappling with the racial justice reckoning sparked by the May 2020 murder of George Floyd coupled with a global pandemic that had lasted over a year, with vaccines only beginning to be distributed and none yet for children. Fairfax County Public Schools (FCPS) were front and center in this firestorm, as COVID-19 tore through our most vulnerable communities. Stressed and overworked parents struggled with supporting their kids in virtual school. Many students were bored, disengaged, lonely and suffering the effects of sedentary isolation. Teachers reported the highest stress levels of their careers as some community members began denigrating FCPS staff and the school board for the long COVID-related school closures. Part of their outrage centered on equity work FCPS undertook in the wake of the Floyd murder. Frustrated parents began counting every penny FCPS put toward righting certain long-standing wrongs while schools remained virtual (for example, removing

Confederate names from schools, bringing in authors and noted speakers to address issues of racial justice for professional development and conducting listening sessions with Black and brown students who endured racial harm in school). Suddenly, this all became a preposterous waste of time, energy and tax dollars to some very angry parents. The "coming together for racial justice" window had long closed by the spring of 2021, and though our government institutions remained committed to the equity work dictated by the One Fairfax policy adopted by our Board of Supervisors, some members of our community seemed to have had enough.

As the Third Vice-President and Education Chair of the Fairfax County NAACP, I had a front-row seat as all this played out in our community. I regularly engage in issues of existing school segregation in Fairfax County (via zip code, "preppable" and expensive standardized testing for gifted and magnet programs, unequal academic/enrichment opportunities throughout the county, et cetera). In fact, my very presence on this library board was the result of fallout from ignorant remarks made during a board meeting regarding the FCPL featured reading list and my public comment regarding those remarks.

So, it was with this sense of awareness about the controversies boiling up in our community regarding race and equity that I posed a question to the Library Foundation staff at that orientation meeting in April 2021: Were the Fairfax County Public Libraries segregated? And if they were, where were there libraries for Black citizens, or were there just no libraries? The staff wasn't sure, but they had not heard about library segregation. It seemed unlikely to me that a community so committed to school segregation, which built and named schools for Confederates as a direct thumbing of the nose to *Brown v. Board of Education*, would have tolerated integrated libraries without a fuss. From that simple query grew this revelatory project. What a story.

LaPierre and Barbuschak answer the question of whether our libraries were segregated (short answer: yes) and the more complicated and nuanced ways a racist school superintendent, W.T. Woodson—for whom we still have a school named—justified the eventual integration of libraries while still steadfastly holding firm on the segregation of schools. With example after example, the absurdity of library segregation is revealed: professional designers needing an art book to design draperies are turned away; a lawyer wanting access to his community library to study is turned way; and a library that is no longer segregated is never visited by the Black community, which would have no way of knowing the library is integrated when the rest of their world is not. The libraries, like the schools, remained segregated long after the law demanded they be integrated, and yet few in our community even know that was ever the case.

This history dives deep into the archives to piece together a story of how protest, resistance and the calculated activism of brave individuals integrated the libraries of Virginia. In these stories, we are reminded of how far we have come. And as book banning again becomes a very real threat, this history also reminds us also of how far we have to go.

My hope is that this story of library desegregation in Fairfax County and the state of Virginia becomes part of the Virginia history taught to our children in school. It is every bit as impactful as the story of school segregation and the slow crawl to integration—and it is a successful story. Our libraries achieved the goal of desegregation where our schools maintain a de facto segregation via countless limitations to equitable access. I am thrilled that a simple question asked offhand, to which I expected the answer to be a plain yes, resulted in this comprehensive history. It is with gratitude and humility that I write this foreword, hoping that all of you find this history as fascinating and informative as I did.

Sujatha Hampton, PhD
Library Board of Trustees, Dranesville District
Fairfax NAACP, Third Vice-President/Education Chair

ACKNOWLEDGEMENTS

A tremendous amount of gratitude goes out to the many people who eagerly supported us as we researched and wrote this book. Our initial thanks go out to the two individuals chiefly responsible for making this book a reality: Dr. Sujatha Hampton and Jessica Hudson. In 2021, Dr. Hampton, a trustee on the Fairfax County Public Library Board, first raised the question about whether Fairfax County Public Library (FCPL) was ever segregated at a board meeting. Library staff in FCPL's Virginia Room had received the same question numerous times over the years, and as best staff could determine, FCPL had always been open to everyone since its establishment in 1939. Dr. Hampton challenged that general response and asked us to dig deeper. Jessica Hudson, the director of FCPL, facilitated that request and asked us to examine the accessibility at other Northern Virginia public libraries during the Jim Crow era. The result of that work is what you now hold in your hands.

Many people assisted us along the way, particularly fellow public librarians. In no specific order, we would like to thank the staff at the Library of Virginia and Library of Congress; Laura Wickstead and Elaine McRey of Fairfax County Public Library's Virginia Room; Donald L. Wilson and Dave Shumate of the Ruth E. Lloyd Information Center (RELIC) of Prince William Public Libraries; the staff of Alexandria Public Library's Special Collections/Local History Branch; Fay Winkle and Audrey Davis of the Alexandria Black History Museum; Laura E. Christiansen of the Thomas Balch Library; Judith Knudsen, Gregory Pierce and John Stanton of Arlington Public Library's Center for Local History; Greg Eatroff of Portsmouth Public Library's Esther Murdaugh Wilson Memorial Room; Derek Gray of the People's Archive at D.C. Public Library; Michael Florer of the Eisenhower National Historic Site; Sonja Woods of the Moorland-Spingarn Research Center, Howard University; and Peter Sullivan, Marshall Webster and, especially, Paula Hawkins of the Mary Riley Styles Library. Paula, who was simultaneously researching the history of segregation at Falls Church's public library, provided invaluable assistance to us.

Thanks to Eugene Scheel, A.J. Roberts, Sylvainia Warner Preston and her mother for sharing memories of the Murrays and helping identify them in a photograph. Others who were incredibly helpful include Aaron Betz, Heather Bollinger, Kay Martin Britto, Elsa Burrowes, Dee Carter, Jeff Clark, Barbara Glakas, Michelle Gullett, Suzanne Levy, Virginia Marshall, Maddy McCoy, Gloria Runyon, Deb Smith-Cohen, Pat Taylor and many more. Thank you to our editor, Kate Jenkins of The History Press, who guided us through the publication process and carried us to the finish line.

On a personal note, Chris would like to thank his mother, Karen Barbuschak, for her unwavering support and for being the best free researcher's assistant and editor in town. Thanks, Mom! Thank you also to his grandparents Michael and Lucy Barbuschak, who tolerated his erratic periods of disappearance to focus on researching and writing this book. His gratitude also goes to Katie Danner for being such an enthusiastic cheerleader throughout this journey.

Suzanne would like to thank her husband, David LaPierre, for joining her on trips to explore sites, meet people and take photographs of landmarks for this book; and her son, Nathan LaPierre, for his encouragement and understanding of the need for this research. She gratefully acknowledges her late parents, Robert and Sherma Summers, for telling her, whenever she griped about injustice, to "write a letter." This is a long letter.

INTRODUCTION

"*We* are staying." Those were the words of nineteen-year-old William "Buddy" Evans as he sat holding a book in the Alexandria Library in Virginia on a hot August Monday in 1939.[1] He addressed the police officer who had just informed him he would be arrested if he refused to leave the library. Like the four other young Black men who entered that day, he was now seated at a table after being denied a library card due to his race. The public library was only open to white residents.

Public libraries are often referred to as bastions of democracy, providing equal access to knowledge and shared resources. In a national survey, 94 percent of adults who have used a public library agreed that "public libraries are welcoming, friendly place(s)."[2]

Yet public libraries have not always been open to all. During the Jim Crow era in the southern United States, many public libraries served white residents only. Black residents often had no public library service at all or were restricted to separate libraries or bookmobile stops. Segregated libraries for Black residents were typically much smaller than those reserved for white residents, often filled with older books that had been discarded from the "main" library.

In the state of Virginia, libraries receiving state aid have been required to provide service to all residents since 1946. This rule was passed into law as chapter 170 of the 1946 Acts of Assembly. The language still appears in the Code of Virginia as § 42.1-55: "The service of books in library systems and libraries receiving state aid shall be free and shall be made available to all persons living in the county, region or municipality."[3]

However, this wording was interpreted by some to mean that segregated libraries or bookmobile deliveries could suffice as service to Black citizens.[4] Other libraries simply ignored the mandate altogether and continued to serve white inhabitants only.

In 1954, with the *Brown v. Board of Education* ruling, the U.S. Supreme Court found "separate-but-equal" unconstitutional. Even after this milestone, many public libraries in Virginia and elsewhere in the South continued to exclude or limit use by Black residents—that is, until Black citizens turned activists launched protests and lawsuits to gain access.

Uniquely situated between the rest of Virginia and the cosmopolitan hub of the nation's capital, Northern Virginia's story of library desegregation is similar yet distinct from that of the rest of the South. Many Black Northern Virginia scholars who lacked access to their neighborhood libraries during segregation relied on Washington, D.C.'s resources. Some parts of Northern Virginia that border the capital city were among the first in the state to integrate public libraries, while others remained segregated as long as those in the Deep South.

While desegregation attempts in some parts of Northern Virginia were well-publicized at the time, like those in the city of Alexandria and Loudoun County, others required a deeper dive into the archives to discover whether the libraries had been segregated and to what extent. Much of the history outlined here, especially that of libraries in Fairfax County, the city of Falls Church and Prince William County, is derived from local archives and has never been published before.

For the purposes of this book, Northern Virginia is defined as the counties and cities bordering Fairfax County, Virginia's most populous county. These include the counties of Arlington, Fairfax, Loudoun and Prince William, as well as the independent cities of Alexandria, Fairfax, Falls Church and Manassas. Examples from elsewhere in Virginia and Washington, D.C., are included for context.

──────── Part I ────────

"We Are Staying"

NORTHERN VIRGINIA

1

CITY OF ALEXANDRIA

We are staying.
—*William "Buddy" Evans*

The city of Alexandria was the site of the earliest publicized resistance to public library segregation in Virginia. The 1939 protest organized by Samuel Wilbert Tucker (1913–1990) was a milestone for civil rights activism. Although it did not result in the library integrating (rather a separate branch was opened for Black residents), Tucker's efforts brought much-needed attention to the injustice of public libraries barring access to citizens based on race.

The roots of Alexandria Library go back to 1794, when it was a private lending library called the Alexandria Library Company. The first branch of what is currently Alexandria Library opened in 1937, when Robert South Barrett donated funds to build a public library in memory of his mother, physician Kate Waller Barrett. This library still stands on Queen Street and is now known as the Barrett Branch. At the time, it was known simply as the Alexandria Library, as it was the only branch.[5]

The library opened in 1937 for "all persons of the white race living in the city of Alexandria and to all persons of the white race who are taxpayers in Alexandria."[6] White people who lived outside Alexandria and did not pay taxes could use the library for a fee of $1.50 a year. Nonwhite taxpayers and residents could not use the library, with or without a fee.[7]

The Alexandria Public Library, built in memory of Dr. Kate Waller Barrett, is seen here only a few days after its construction was finished in August 1937. *D.C. Public Library, Star Collection* © Washington Post.

This was unacceptable to Samuel W. Tucker, a young lawyer who lived only a block and a half from the library but who had been denied use of it due to his race. In addition to legal action, he masterminded a protest that would be one of the first sit-ins of the civil rights movement.[8]

SAMUEL WILBERT TUCKER

Born and raised in Alexandria, Tucker was a gifted student. His mother was a teacher, and his father was a charter member of Alexandria's NAACP. As a child, Samuel had been tutored in the law by his father's colleague Tom Watson, and by age fourteen, he had written deeds and helped prepare clients for court.[9] Tucker passed the bar exam at the age of twenty, a few months after his graduation from Howard University, without ever attending law school. He had to wait until he was twenty-one, however, to begin practicing law. (He studied for the bar exam at the D.C. Public Library and Library of Congress, both of which were open to people of all races.)

Now twenty-six, Tucker devised a two-fold strategy to gain access to Alexandria's library: he initiated legal maneuvers, as well as a public protest designed to gain publicity. Tucker accompanied his neighbor George Wilson,

An Alexandria native, attorney Samuel Wilbert Tucker, launched a lawsuit and protest in a historic attempt to desegregate Alexandria Library in 1939. *Alexandria Black History Museum.*

a retired U.S. Army sergeant, to the library and attempted to apply for a library card for Wilson. The request was denied due to Wilson's race.[10] Tucker filed suit, citing that all Alexandrians who paid taxes should have access to the publicly funded facility.

While waiting for the results from his lawsuit, Tucker also planned the now-famous sit-in. Tucker recruited five young men between the ages of eighteen and twenty-two, as well as a fourteen-year-old lookout, Robert "Bobby" Strange. (Originally, there were eleven participants, but only five showed up for the event, probably due to family concerns for their safety.) The men who appeared on that fateful day were William "Buddy" Evans, Edward Gaddis, Morris Murray, Clarence Strange and Otto Tucker (Samuel's younger brother).

On Monday, August 21, 1939, the five men—smartly attired and well mannered—entered one at a time and requested library cards. Each was denied based on their race; after this, each proceeded to take a book from the shelves and sit quietly at separate tables in the library to read. When the young men declined to leave, police were called, and they informed the men that they could be arrested if they did not leave. Evans replied that they would stay.

The young lookout ran to alert Tucker that police were on their way, and Tucker notified the press. Reporters and photographers arrived in time to record the arrest of the protesters, and news of this spread via newspapers in several states throughout the country.[11]

The sit-in participants were charged with trespassing. In his capacity as a lawyer, Tucker argued that, as citizens, the men had a right to be in a public building and thus were not trespassing. Their charges were lowered to disorderly conduct. Tucker argued successfully that skin color alone was not enough to constitute disorderly conduct, as the men had been polite and well dressed. Ultimately, the case was buried by the judge; the young men were not convicted and did not serve jail time.

The case raised hope within the Black community that libraries throughout the region would be integrated. "The decision, in all probability, means that all public libraries in the South, which now bar colored, can be

Alexandria Library protesters are escorted from the library by police and placed under arrest on August 21, 1939. *Alexandria Black History Museum.*

forced to admit them," reported the *Baltimore Afro-American* newspaper.[12] But the protest did not result in the library being integrated. Instead, a separate library for Black residents was hastily built, opening less than a year later. Robert H. Robinson Library, located at 638 North Alfred Street, opened on April 24, 1940. The Robinson Library was smaller, open for fewer hours and had older books. The librarian, who was Black, was paid half the salary of the white librarian at the Queen Street branch.[13]

Records show that the city's library board had discussed the "question of a Colored library" as early as March 1937, before the Queens Street library opened in August that year, but no action had been taken.[14] The board renewed its discussions shortly before Tucker's attempt to procure a library card for Wilson, debating options such as expanding the library at the Parker-Gray School (a segregated school for Black students), building an annex onto the white-only library (with or without a separate entrance) or erecting a new building.[15] Tucker's litigation lit a fire under officials to take action.

Above: The exterior of the Robert Robinson Library, circa the 1940s. *Alexandria Black History Museum.*

Right: Librarian Sarah M. Carr stands at the entrance of Robinson Library, circa the 1940s. *Alexandria Black History Museum.*

Courts dragged out the case against the young protesters, as well as the petition for Wilson to be granted a library card, in an apparent attempt to get plans for a separate library for Black citizens underway to justify the denial of services at the Queen Street library.

Tucker was disgusted with the "solution" of a separate library, refusing to accept a library card issued for the "Colored library," as it was known, and not the library near his home. He sent a letter to a librarian at the Queen Street branch dated February 13, 1940:

> *I refuse and will always refuse to accept a card to be used at the library to be constructed and operated at Alfred and Wythe Streets in lieu of a card to be used at the existing library on Queen Street, for which I have made an application. Continued delay—beyond the close of this month—in issuing to me a card for use at the library on Queen Street will be taken as a refusal to do so, whereupon I will feel justified in seeking the aid of court to enforce my right.*[16]

However, illness sidelined Tucker from continuing the fight, and during this time, plans were approved for two segregated libraries.

Perhaps Tucker anticipated how inferior the library for Black residents would be compared to the Queen Street facility. His sister Elsie Thomas described this contrast in the documentary film *Out of Obscurity*: "When you compare the Queen Street Library with Robert Robinson Library, it was like comparing the mansion to the slave quarters."[17] Despite this inequity, many Black Alexandrians, especially children, made eager use of the new resource.[18]

The desegregation of Alexandria's public libraries eventually occurred in phases between 1959 and 1962. According to historian Dr. Brenda Mitchell-Powell:

> *The Robinson Library continued to serve the needs of African American Alexandrians, despite acknowledged overcrowded conditions, until February 1959. That winter, the Alexandria Library quietly integrated for African American adults and high school students. Children continued to be served by the Robinson Library until July 1962, when the Alexandria Library was fully integrated.*[19]

The Robinson Library building currently houses the Alexandria Black History Museum.

Story time in the Robinson Library Branch, 1950. *Alexandria Library, Special Collections.*

Now widely recognized as a civil rights trailblazer, Tucker continued to work on behalf of equality throughout his life, battling school segregation and running for Congress twice to encourage Black citizens to vote. He served as a lead lawyer for the NAACP in Virginia, appearing before the U.S. Supreme Court several times, and was a founding partner in the Richmond law firm Hill, Tucker and Marsh. Having served in the military during World War II, he was buried in Arlington National Cemetery.

On October 18, 2019, the Alexandria Circuit Court dismissed all charges against the sit-in participants. Although the five young Black men recruited by Tucker had been charged with disorderly conduct, the court found that they were "lawfully exercising their constitutional rights of free assembly and speech and the right to petition the government to alter the established policy of sanctioned segregation at the time of their arrest.…Sitting peacefully in a library reading books…was not in any fashion disorderly or likely to cause acts of violence."[20]

Sarah M. Carr, librarian, inside Robinson Library. *Alexandria Black History Museum.*

Gladys Davis helping customers in the Barrett branch, 1965. Davis began her career in the segregated Robinson Library. She served Alexandria's library system for sixty years. *Alexandria Library, Special Collections.*

RECOGNITION

Ten years after Tucker's death in 1990, Samuel Tucker Elementary School was dedicated in honor of his legacy. His sister Elsie V. Thomas was present for the school's October 2000 opening ceremony, during which his portrait was hung in the school. The keynote speaker at the event was Lyndia Person Ramsey, a deputy commonwealth attorney of Sussex County, Virginia, who had been represented by Tucker in a school desegregation case as a child. The school stands at 435 Ferdinand Day Drive in Alexandria.

Alexandria Library has regular anniversary events to commemorate Tucker's historic sit-in. In August 2019, for the eightieth anniversary of the protest, all branches of the system hosted remembrance events. Several descendants of the 1939 activists participated and were featured on READ posters. In 2022, the Library of Virginia named Samuel Tucker among its "Strong Men and Women of Virginia" in observation of Black History Month.[21]

EXISTING SITES AND LANDMARKS

Alexandria Black History Museum
902 Wythe Street, Alexandria, VA 22314

The original Robinson Library is now the Alexandria Black History Museum. *Authors' photograph.*

Completed in 1940, the Robert H. Robinson Library was built as a segregated facility to serve Black residents of the city of Alexandria. After integration, from 1962 until 1969, the Robinson Library served as the city's bookmobile station. The building was reopened as the Alexandria Black History Research Center in 1983, and in 2004, it was renamed the Alexandria Black History Museum. A plaque mounted on a concrete panel commemorating the Robert Robertson Library can be found on the museum's grounds at the southwest intersection of North Alfred and Wythe Streets.

Kate Waller Barrett Branch Library
717 Queen Street, Alexandria, VA 22314

Built in 1937, the Barrett branch was the site of the August 21, 1939 sit-in organized by attorney Samuel Tucker in an attempt to desegregate the

library. A plaque commemorating the protest, erected in March 2000, can be found in the lobby. An outdoor historical marker detailing the events surrounding the sit-in greets visitors across from the front entrance. In 2020, a state historical marker titled "Alexandria Library Sit-In" was erected around the corner from the branch on North Washington Street.

This page, top: The City of Alexandria placed this commemorative plaque inside the Barrett branch in 2000. *Authors' photograph.*

This page, bottom: The original Alexandria Library, now known as the Kate Waller Barrett Branch, has been in use for over eighty-five years. *Authors' photograph.*

Following page: Erected in 2020, this state historical marker commemorating the 1939 library sit-in is visible to passing motorists on North Washington Street. *Authors' photograph.*

27

ARLINGTON COUNTY

*T*oday's Arlington Public Library was predated by several small community libraries. Most of these, like almost 75 percent of the early libraries in the United States, were started by women's clubs.[22] Due to segregated neighborhoods, separate churches and social clubs, such community libraries were typically implicitly if not explicitly segregated in Virginia into the mid-twentieth century.

The Carrie M. Rohrer Library was started in 1915 by members of the Ladies Guild of the Vanderwerken Congregational Church. It was the only public library in Arlington County at that time. The women organized the library in memory of a young mother who had died, raising "outside" funds by selling Christmas cards and handcrafted items. The library moved to Rock Spring Congregational Church in 1940 and was moved into an attached room built for the purpose of holding a library in 1954. By the 1950s, the books had been cataloged according to the Dewey Decimal System, and the library's circulation amounted to about 6,700 books per year.[23] Though the library was invited to join Arlington Public Library during its inception, it remained independent. Now known as Rohrer Memorial Library, it still operates from the church on the corner of Little Falls and Rock Springs Roads.

In 1923, the Burdett Library opened as the first freestanding public library in Arlington. This library had its roots in the Glencarlyn community, dating to the late 1800s with the personal book collection of former Union Civil War general and Missouri congressman Samuel Burdett. Burdett lived in Arlington for twenty-five years until his death in 1914. "His home on the northeast corner across from the library was the most pretentious in the village....His wife, his niece, a parrot and a dog made up his family.

He had a large horse, Moses, which was pastured in the block east of the library," a neighbor wrote of his life.[24] The general bequeathed his personal collection to Arlington County, along with an endowment fund to grow the collection into a public library.

In 1936, five community libraries—Glencarlyn, Cherrydale, Clarendon, Aurora Hills and Arlington (later Columbia Pike Library)—merged to form Arlington County Library Association. The next year, an official "libraries" department with a designated budget and director became part of the Arlington County government. However, these library branches only provided service to white residents.[25]

THE HOLMES LIBRARY ASSOCIATION AND HOLMES BRANCH

Black residents of Arlington mobilized to create the Henry Louis Holmes Library Association in 1940. Although the group was formed primarily to serve Black residents during segregation, the organization's constitution, dated August 23, 1940, reads: "The object of this association shall be to own and maintain a free public library.…Any individual who is interested in the library may become a member by making it known and participating in the work of the association."[26]

The first president of Holmes Library Association was Kitty Bruce, a chairwoman of the Arlington Inter-Racial Commission and teacher at Francis Junior High School in Washington, D.C., a school for Black children. The organization's board of directors included Reverend A. Mackley of Mount Olive Baptist Church and Nora Drew, the mother of pioneering surgeon Dr. Charles Drew. Early members of the association came from the Civic Association of Halls Hill, the Nauck neighborhood and the Jennie Dean Club.

The Holmes Library Association received no government funding. Books were donated by the Alpha Gamma and Iota Chi Lambda sororities and other civic groups. Some supplies were donated from the Clarendon Library Association.[27] Space for the library was provided by two local churches consecutively. In 1940, the library found a home in the basement of Mount Olive Baptist Church, at 700 South Arlington Ridge Road. In 1942, it moved to the basement of Lomax AME Zion Church at 2706 South Twenty-Fourth Street.[28]

The library and the organization that founded it were named after Henry Louis Holmes, whose portrait hung in the library. Holmes was a prominent Arlington civic leader who served as commissioner of revenue from 1877 to 1904. Once enslaved, Holmes had moved to Freedman's Village in Arlington, where he worked as a farmer and laborer while becoming prominent in Reconstruction-era politics. In 1879, along with William H. Butler, he purchased land and began to develop what would become the Butler-Holmes community, now the Penrose neighborhood.[29]

In 1944, Holmes Library joined Arlington Public Library as a branch. It moved to the George Washington Carver Homes complex at Thirteenth Street South and South Queen Street, where it finally had its own small freestanding building. Painted white with striped awnings over the windows, the library bore a sign over its door proclaiming, "Public Library/Holmes Branch." Its Black staff members over the years included Marie Louise Owens, branch librarian, and Arthur McLaurin, library assistant.[30]

The county board appropriated $2,100 toward the library, which helped make possible the addition of books—2,500 at opening.[31] Although the collection was by far the smallest of any Arlington branch, Holmes Library flourished in its new location, which was convenient to the residents of

Holmes Branch Library as it appeared in 1946, when it was located in the George Washington Carver Homes complex as a branch of the Arlington Public Library. *Center for Local History, Arlington Public Library.*

The interior of Holmes Branch Library, with a librarian and two children, in 1946. *Center for Local History, Arlington Public Library.*

Carver Homes. Carver Homes began as a Federal Public Housing Authority project in 1943 to house people displaced during the construction of the Pentagon. Originally composed of trailers and one hundred temporary public-financed housing units, it later developed into an eight-building apartment complex. Sadly, in 1949, the property on which the library stood was sold by the government. Holmes Library was again without a home.

While this was a blow for the library, on another level, the sale of the property represented progress for the Black community. The property was purchased by two Black-owned cooperatives that had been formed by tenants of Carver Homes: Paul Laurence Dunbar and George Washington Carver Mutual Associations. These were the first two Black-owned cooperatives in the United States. Their purchase of the property helped preserve affordable housing for Black residents, which was in short supply during segregation.[32]

Arlington Public Library Desegregates

In 1950, still unable to find an alternate location for the former Holmes Branch, Arlington Public Library quietly integrated its libraries. Arlington Public Library's website states:

> The first mention of desegregation appears in the Library Department Annual Report for 1949–1950. Under the heading "Library Service for Colored Citizens," it reported, "In January 1950, lacking a branch library for the colored citizens, the county manager approved the use of all branches by all residents of the county." This was also listed as the date of desegregation in a 1964 report from the Community Council for Social Progress, and mention of library service for colored citizens does not appear in any subsequent annual reports, beyond mention of circulation statistics for the Hoffman-Boston library deposit station.[33]

While it is not specified in the records, it's most likely that the decision to desegregate was made to comply with the 1946 Code of Virginia law requiring libraries receiving state aid to serve all residents. It is unclear whether any attempt was made to notify Black residents that they were now free to use—let alone welcome to use—formerly segregated branches. Since the school system was not desegregated until 1959 and the county's parks and recreation facilities were not desegregated until 1962, it is likely that without a formal effort to invite the Black community to library branches, Black residents might assume they were still excluded. Oral history interviews with residents from the time, such as civil rights activist Dorothy Hamm, indicate that Black residents of Arlington believed they did not have access to public libraries.[34]

After the Holmes Branch Library closed, its books were stored in the hopes that a new location could be found. Eventually, the stored collection was used to supply other branches. "These books were in a storage shed in back of Clarendon Library. One of my early jobs was to take a flashlight—it didn't have lights—to get duplicate copies of things we needed in the library system from this Holmes Branch group of books," recalled Jane Nida, who became the first assistant director of Arlington Public Library in November 1954.[35] The children's books went to the Hoffman-Boston School, where they were needed to make those library facilities acceptable to the state.[36]

Hoffman-Boston School was the only secondary school for Black students in Arlington until the public school system desegregated in 1959. It was built in 1915, replacing the Jefferson School, Arlington's first school for Black

The only library available to Black Arlington students prior to the opening of the Holmes Library was the school library of Hoffman-Boston High School, shown here in the 1950s. *Center for Local History, Arlington Public Library.*

children that was opened in 1870. Hoffman-Boston School remained open until its last students graduated in 1964. Prior to the Holmes Library, the only library available to many Black children in Arlington was the Hoffman-Boston school library.

Mildred Johnson served as the long-term school librarian of Hoffman-Boston. The school's library was also used by the Black community, according to Nida: "They had a very good school library and a very good school librarian—and the Black community, I do believe, used that more frequently [than the public library]."[37]

With the closing of the Holmes Branch and the subsequent declaration that all branches were integrated, Arlington became the first county in Virginia to desegregate a formerly segregated library system, albeit without controversy or fanfare. The silence of the process, however, meant that Black residents had little way of knowing they were now able to use libraries that had been formerly white-only.

Arlington County and the city of Alexandria both border Washington, D.C., as the northernmost parts of Virginia, so why did Arlington Public Library integrate early while Alexandria Library was among the last to do

Students at work inside the Hoffman-Boston High School library, circa 1950. *Center for Local History, Arlington Public Library.*

Mildred Johnson, a long-term librarian at the Hoffman-Boston High School library, as pictured in the school's 1962 yearbook. *Center for Local History, Arlington Public Library.*

so? The presence of the Robinson branch enabled Alexandria to forestall full integration until 1962, while Arlington was compelled to integrate in 1950 by the loss of the Holmes Branch in 1949. This is an example of how the presence of segregated facilities for Black residents delayed full integration. While many segregated libraries for the Black community, like the Holmes Library, were started by Black residents to provide resources otherwise inaccessible to them, there were also white supporters of segregation, whether they were private individuals or government entities, who lobbied for segregated facilities as a means of forestalling integration.

Recognition

An annex to Arlington County Courthouse was named in honor of Henry Louis Holmes in recognition of his service as the commissioner of revenue, but that building has since been demolished. The portrait of Holmes that once hung in Holmes Library currently hangs in the office of the commissioner of revenue at the Ellen M. Bozman Government Center in Arlington. Arlington's Butler Holmes Park, named after the pioneering landowners, is located within the original Butler Holmes subdivision at 101 South Barton Street. In 2022, Arlington Public Library created a webpage about Henry Louis Holmes Library, making public original documents related to the library and its founders.

Existing Sites and Landmarks

Penrose Neighborhood
Central Arlington, VA 22204

Penrose, a thriving commuter neighborhood three miles from Washington, D.C., grew from land purchased in 1879 and subdivided in 1882 by William Butler and Henry Louis Holmes. Many descendants of original residents still live

Penrose neighborhood, once known as the Butler Holmes Subdivision, has been home to members of the Holmes and Butler families for generations. *Authors' photograph.*

there. A house at what was once 2803 South Second Street (now absorbed into another property) was occupied by Holmes's widow until she died in the 1960s. Holmes family members left the ownership of the house to "Miss Carol," who ran a restaurant for Black customers out of the property during segregation.[38] A Queen Anne–style home constructed by Butler still stands at 2407 South Second Street as of this writing.

Signage marks the former home of Charles Drew, the first Black recipient of a doctor of science degree in medicine. His mother, Nora Drew, helped establish Holmes Library in Arlington. *Authors' photograph.*

The Drew House
2505 South First Street, Arlington, VA 22204

Dr. Charles Drew, a pioneering Black surgeon whose research led to modern-day blood banking, lived in the Butler Holmes community now known as Penrose. As head of surgery at Howard University, he protested the racial segregation of blood donations. Drew's 1910-era home, where he lived until 1939, is a designated National Historic Landmark and is still occupied by members of the Drew family. The Holmes Library Board of Directors included Nora Drew, Dr. Drew's mother. Her daughter Nora Drew Gregory later served on the board of trustees of the D.C. Public Library.[39]

3

FAIRFAX COUNTY

*I*n 1962, Bernice Lloyd Bell, a library student at Atlanta University in Georgia, began working on her thesis for her master of science in library service degree. Bell sought to discover if progress had been made in making public library facilities available to Black residents in thirteen southern states since two similar surveys had been conducted in 1953. She sent out questionnaires to 290 libraries around the country, including 33 library systems in Virginia, asking a range of questions concerning integration. The results were incorporated into her August 1963 unpublished thesis, "Integration in Public Library Service in Thirteen Southern States, 1954–1962."

Fairfax County Public Library (FCPL), established in 1939, was one of the library systems that responded to her survey. Although the completed six-page questionnaire, likely answered by FCPL director Mary K. McCulloch, no longer exists, Bell compiled some of the responses into a table of statistics. According to the questionnaire, FCPL responded as always being open to all races.

The 1954 Supreme Court case *Brown v. Board of Education*, which overruled the "separate but equal" doctrine, had no influence on FCPL's decision to open library facilities, as they were already open to everyone by then. According to FCPL, it was generally known that Black citizens had free access to the library and its branches; however, no special efforts were made to inform those residents of the services available. FCPL also included books by Black authors in its collections but did not subscribe to Black special interest magazines.[40]

Although FCPL positively responded to Bell's survey as always being open to all races, this was in fact not always the case. The Fairfax County Public Library Board of Trustees agreed to serve the Black residents of the county at one of its first board meetings in 1940; however, segregated service and limiters were in place from the beginning.

Early Libraries in Fairfax County

Prior to the establishment of FCPL in 1939, individual communities and towns in Fairfax County formed their own libraries without any professional assistance. There were at least six known small libraries: Fortnightly Club Library of Herndon (1889), Vienna Town Library (1897), Falls Church Library (1899), McLean Community Library (1915), Fairfax County Library (1929) and the Forestville (Great Falls) Community Library (1938). All but Vienna Town Library eventually partnered with FCPL to serve as community libraries. Additionally, a few churches, schools and clubs maintained small circulating libraries, including the Annandale School (1904), Great Falls Episcopal Church (1933), Church of the Holy Comforter in Vienna (1936) and Vale Club (1937).

While founding charters, bylaws and constitutional documents no longer survive for most of the six community libraries, by the time they partnered with FCPL in 1939 as unofficial branches, documentation confirms that all of them served only the white residents of Fairfax County. In time, all the communities that had these volunteer-run libraries received their own FCPL branches. Of the six original libraries, two officially transitioned to become FCPL branches: Dolley Madison in McLean (1956) and Herndon Fortnightly (1971).

Fortnightly Club and Library Association of Herndon

The Fortnightly Club of Herndon, one of the oldest federated women's clubs in Virginia, organized the first library in the county in 1889. The group was originally founded as a study club, with forty books in its collection; this collection eventually grew to comprise more than one thousand volumes.[41] The library formally opened to the public on May 28, 1900, and during its regular hours of operation, it was reported to be "free to all."[42] The library was destroyed during the town of Herndon's Great Fire of 1917, but the Fortnightly Club quickly rebuilt the collection with insurance money. The Good Templars donated toward the construction of a permanent building, and the library opened in the new space in early 1927.

When the library incorporated in 1925 as the Fortnightly Club and Library Association, its charter made no mention of segregationist policies. However, when the library partnered with FCPL as a community library, FCPL circulation reports dating to the 1940s confirm that the Herndon Fortnightly Library maintained a "whites only" policy. In May 2021, Barbara Glakas of the Herndon Historical Society spoke to twelve long-time residents of Herndon to gauge their recollections on whether the library had indeed been segregated.

One white resident, a woman in her late seventies who attended school in Herndon, recalled the library being segregated in the 1950s. Other white residents who Glakas interviewed did not recall if it was segregated; however,

A group of children pose in front of the Herndon Fortnightly Club's library in 1962. This building, built in 1927 to house the library after the original structure burned to the ground, was leased to Fairfax County Public Library in 1971. *D.C. Public Library, Star Collection* © Washington Post.

half of them told her, "It probably was since so many other things were segregated in town."[43] The town of Herndon itself was generally segregated well into the 1960s.

Glakas also interviewed a ninety-three-year-old Black woman who grew up in Oak Grove, a historically Black community in Herndon. She moved to the area in 1939 and recalled, "I never went to that library," because she "never tried or wanted to go. We knew not to." She remembered that the Oak Grove School's teachers lived in nearby Vienna and Washington, D.C., and said they would bring books to the school for the children to use.[44] The Herndon Fortnightly Library officially joined the FCPL system in July 1971.

VIENNA TOWN LIBRARY

The Vienna Town Library, a small square clapboard building originally located at Library Lane and Maple Avenue, was the town's first public library, erected in 1897. The building was moved to the corner of Center Street Southeast and Maple Avenue in 1912.[45] When the Vienna Library Association incorporated on November 7, 1913, it recorded its purpose was "to establish and maintain a circulating library for the use and benefit of the white inhabitants of said town and vicinity."[46]

The Vienna Town Library, seen here in the early 1960s, was open to only white citizens. *FCPL Photographic Archive.*

The Vienna Library Association fiercely resisted pressure to integrate during the 1950s, which led to the creation of the "Friends of the Library Vienna, Virginia," in 1958. The friends' efforts to have a library in town that equally provided materials and services to all residents culminated with the opening of FCPL's Patrick Henry branch in 1962.

The First "County Library" in Fairfax County

Before FCPL's formation in 1939, a Fairfax County Library was already in existence. In November 1929, at the request of Thomas R. Keith and Professor Ormond Stone, the Fairfax County Board of Supervisors gave approval for a room in the Old Clerk's Office Building on the Fairfax Courthouse grounds to be used as a county library. However, the board stipulated that the county would have no connection to or responsibility for the library, nor would it provide the library with financial assistance.[47] During its decade-long existence, the library was known as the Fairfax County Library, but it was never officially designated as such.

In early February 1930, a committee of citizens formed the Fairfax County Library Association, electing Mrs. Milton D. Hall, the wife of the former superintendent of Fairfax County Public Schools, president.[48] The Association reached out to the community for financial assistance and donations of furniture, shelving and books to create the library. The Fairfax County Colored Citizens Association also tried to help establish the library by obtaining funds from the county school board in 1931.[49]

Initially, the Fairfax County Library was intended to be subscription based. Library cards were sent out to citizens requesting annual dues: an active membership cost one dollar, a contributing membership cost five dollars and a sustaining membership cost twenty-five dollars. However, by the time the library finally opened in 1932, the association provided free services with an optional sustaining membership. Private donations entirely supported the library, and the association appointed Lydia Palmer as its volunteer librarian.

After nearly three years of effort, the Fairfax County Library opened on Friday, July 25, 1932, and remained open from 2:00 to 5:00 p.m. The facility consisted of two rooms: a reading area and the old vault of the clerk's office, which housed the books.[50] The entire book collection was donated by Fairfax County citizens. Despite receiving support from the Fairfax County Colored Citizens Association, the library seemed to bar Black citizens all together.

The first Fairfax County Library opened on the second floor of the old clerk's office in 1932. *FCPL Photographic Archive.*

"Any white resident of Fairfax County is entitled to borrow books or use the library as a reading room during these hours," reported the *Fairfax Herald* upon the library's grand opening.[51]

Subsequently, the County Library became somewhat nomadic, moving no less than five times. In 1934, the library was forced to relocate to the basement of a county building because the Old Clerk's Office Building was torn down.[52] The library moved again in 1935 to the second floor of the new Trial Justice Building.[53] In March 1938, the Board of Supervisors ordered the library to vacate its quarters again. It moved into the second-floor auditorium of the old Fairfax Elementary School (now Fairfax Museum and Visitor Center), which was previously the meeting hall for the local Ku Klux Klan (KKK) chapter, the Cavaliers of Virginia.[54] It moved one final time later that year to Old Town Hall.

By 1938, Lydia Palmer had developed the library from its humble beginnings into a well-equipped repository of 4,500 books without any assistance from the county.[55] That February, she appeared before the Board of Supervisors to request that they include an appropriation for the Fairfax County Library in the 1939 budget. The county attorney reported that after reviewing state law, the board first needed to establish a free countywide library system, and the circuit court had to appoint a library board of trustees before making an appropriation of county funds.[56] In light of these facts, the Fairfax County Chamber of Commerce organized a county library committee to petition the Board of Supervisors for the creation of a county free library system.

Town of Fairfax Library

With the establishment of the Fairfax County Public Library system in February 1939, the Original County Library, which finally had a permanent home in Old Town Hall in Fairfax, was reorganized as the Town of Fairfax Library. Joseph E. Willard, a politician and local resident, had built Old Town Hall in 1900 and gifted it to the town. He stipulated five conditions in the July 1900 deed when he transferred the building to the care of trustees; one of these stipulations was that "the use of said hall [was] to be restricted to white people."[57]

This spirit of white privilege continued in June 1939, when the Fairfax Town Library Association formed and elected officers.[58] A draft constitution written by outgoing association president John S. Barbour outlined the association's purpose: "The establishment and maintenance of a free public library in the town of Fairfax for the benefit of white citizens of the town and community and of rendering friendly assistance to any like association organized by and for [our] colored citizens."[59] The association voted to adopt the constitution at its meeting on December 15, 1939.[60] Lydia Palmer, the original librarian of the County Library, continued to serve as librarian until retiring in 1940.

In 1962, despite being overshadowed by the new $680,000 FCPL Headquarters Library erected a block north, Fairfax Town Library

Old Town Hall, seen here in 1966, provided a home on its second floor for the Huddleson Memorial Library. *FCPL Photographic Archive.*

was renamed the Huddleson Memorial Library in honor of Nellie H. Huddleson, a cofounder of the Herndon Fortnightly Library and early supporter of the County Library. The library still exists today on the second floor of Old Town Hall.

Fairfax County Public Library (FCPL)
Is Established

After nearly a decade of effort to create a permanent county library, the Fairfax County Board of Supervisors voted to establish a county free library system on February 1, 1939. With this motion, the Fairfax County Public Library system was born. The board requested that the judge of the circuit court appoint a library board of five trustees from local citizens. One of the trustees was required by law to be the superintendent of public schools.[61] The first board members appointed were: John F. Bethune, Ruth B. Hatch, Kitty Pozer, Kathryn Robinson and Superintendent Wilbert T. Woodson. These original trustees were responsible for creating and directing the policies and operations of the library system.

In March 1939, the Board of Supervisors reluctantly budgeted $250 to fund the library.[62] Because that amount was insufficient for the library's operation, the trustees solicited assistance from the state library board

Completed in 1940, this cinderblock building was the original home of Fairfax County Public Library. *FCPL Photographic Archive.*

and the federal Works Progress Administration (WPA). The WPA agreed to make Fairfax County Public Library a demonstration statewide library project. Under those terms, the WPA supported the loan of a bookmobile with one thousand books and financed the book collection and the salaries for the bookmobile driver, county librarian and additional personnel.[63] The existing community libraries of Fairfax, Falls Church, Forestville (Great Falls), Herndon, McLean and, for a brief time later, Lorton, agreed to support the project by loaning their books for circulation. In return, books from FCPL would be deposited at the cooperating community libraries by the bookmobile.

The library board of trustees appointed John S. Mehler as the system's first county librarian in June 1940.[64] When the WPA bookmobile arrived in Fairfax the following month, FCPL held a welcoming ceremony on the Fairfax Courthouse's green on July 30, 1940. The ceremony was attended by R. Walton Moore, members of the Board of Supervisors and the circuit court and other public officials.[65] The bookmobile's service started almost immediately, using books loaned from the WPA, state library and participating community libraries.

Because the WPA required the bookmobile to be housed in a garage, the Fairfax County Board of Supervisors agreed to build a twenty-four-by-twenty-four-foot cinderblock library building with bookshelves and an attached garage for $1,090 in June 1940.[66] Its construction was completed later that summer. The building was not publicly accessible and served only as a headquarters for the bookmobile and library staff for the next decade.

FCPL Extends Service to Black Residents

At the third meeting of the library board of trustees on September 11, 1939, the trustees met with representatives of existing community libraries and discussed how they could all cooperate. A series of numbered statements from the meeting were recorded by Chairman John F. Bethune, and one of them said, "Books allocated and marked for colored readers will not be available to white readers, and vice versa."[67] However, these numbered statements were not recorded in the official library board of trustees' minutes and only survive because John S. Barbour, the president of Fairfax Library Committee, retained them in his law office files.

No further discussion about offering service to Black residents occurred until the eighth meeting of the library board of trustees on July 22, 1940.

This was the board's second meeting since the hiring of the county librarian. The first topic of discussion was County Librarian Mehler's suggestion that FCPL provide service to Black residents. One of the questions posed was: If it was to be offered, what type and how much service should be provided? The board's minutes record they agreed to offer it:

> *Under the setup of this project, negroes should be served. As none of the books from the various community libraries will be available for negro service, other books will have to be provided. The Extension Division State Library can furnish four hundred children's books, one hundred books for children of high school age and fifty books for adults. Whether these will be sufficient, we will have to wait until operations start to see.*[68]

Despite approving service to Black residents, the question came up again five months later at the library board of trustees meeting on December 10, 1940. By then, Mehler had just retired as county librarian in November, and the board appointed Dorothea C. Asher as his replacement. The minutes reported:

> *The subject of service to negroes was discussed, and it was agreed that this service should be established in Fairfax. Books for negro use have been loaned by the Virginia State Library Extension Division.*[69]

Asher established a Fairfax "Colored" deposit station and made a contact to establish a Falls Church "Colored" station by the following meeting on January 14, 1941.[70] Typically, FCPL's deposit stations were placed in either homes or stores, and the bookmobile made deliveries on a monthly schedule. During its first month of operation, the Fairfax "Colored" station had four adults and two children register as borrowers, and they checked out nine adult and two juvenile fiction titles.[71]

The Falls Church "Colored" station was up and running by the following library board meeting on February 11, 1941.[72] The exact locations and conditions of these two deposit stations remain unknown. Herbert O. Blunt, the Fairfax County correspondent for the *Alexandria Gazette*, reported that April:

> *The bookmobile now makes 46 service stops. Two of the deposit stations serve Negro communities. The library now has a list of 1,400 registered borrowers, with a steady demand for additional service.*[73]

County Librarian Dorothea Asher and library board chairman John F. Bethune visit Major W.H. Hitchcock with the FCPL Bookmobile at Fort Belvoir in 1941. *FCPL Photographic Archive.*

Despite the increasing demand from citizens, Black residents of the county had access to library books through only those two deposit stations. Conversely, white residents could obtain library books and register for library cards through multiple bookmobile stops, deposit stations, school library branches and community library branches that were conveniently placed around the county.

As the county librarian, Dorothea Asher was required to submit detailed weekly work reports to the state library in Richmond. She meticulously chronicled her daily tasks; the bookmobile routes she traveled; the conditions of bookmobile stops, stations and community libraries; individuals and groups she met with; and her personal observations and opinions about the library system. Some of her entries describe how she interacted with the local Black community:

> *Saturday, January 4, 1941: Made fire; interviewed two women about a colored deposit.*

> *Monday, January 13, 1941: Fairfax Town Library—appointment with Mrs. Sweet and talked to her about the negro deposit in Fairfax....Took colored deposit.*

> *Thursday, February 27, 1941: Deposit to Falls Church colored station.*

> *Saturday, May 17, 1941: Went to Arlington to try to see about a worker for a colored unit. Saw the library, but the person in charge teaches in Washington.*

> *Thursday, June 6, 1941: Made Fairfax colored deposit.*[74]

Surviving library records do not indicate whether additional bookmobile deposit stations or stops were established specifically for the Black community. By 1945, "Colored" deposit stations appear to have been discontinued altogether. In April that year, FCPL undertook a thorough reorganization of its bookmobile service under Margaret Edwards, the new county librarian appointed by the library board in 1944. She eliminated many stations and stops and set a definite arrival and departure time for each. The 1945–46 bookmobile schedule no longer listed the Fairfax and Falls Church "Colored" stations or any new segregated stations or stops.

If this was the case, Black residents were not provided any library service by FCPL for a few years in the early 1940s. In addition to not being able to access a book deposit station or the bookmobile itself, those residents also lacked access to the independent community libraries. Surviving FCPL monthly records of circulation, registration and book stock for partnering community libraries confirm this. The monthly record form had a prompt asking whether service was provided to white residents, Black residents or

Form 45
Rev. IV

MONTHLY RECORD
CIRCULATION, REGISTRATION BOOK STOCK

For Deposit Stations (Schools and community
libraries, stores, homes, etc.) where
WPA workers are not employed, or
where total circulation is not
reported on WPA Form 410

_____
Name of demonstration area

Name of station __Forestville, Va.__ Month_____January, 1943_____

Service to: _White_ White
(Indicate whether white, negro, or both)

Type of   Community Library
Station Community Library
(School, store, community library, etc.)

#	ADULT		JUVENILE		TOTAL
	Fiction	Non-Fiction	Fiction	Non Fiction	
1					
2					
3					
4					
5					
6					
7					
8					
9					
10					
11					
12					
13					
14					
15					
16					
17					
18					
19					
20					
21					
22					
23					
24					
25					
26					
27					
28					
29					
30					
31	14	2			16
Total					16

BORROWER REGISTRATION

WHITE	Reported last month	New this month	Total
Adult	89	1	90
Juvenile			
Total			90

NEGRO			
Adult			
Juvenile	/////////////		
Total			
		TOTAL	

INVENTORY

(Books permanently located here)

On hand first of month	During Month			On hand at end of month
	Donated	Purchased	Otherwise discarded	
631	2	-	-	633
				633

Prepare in Duplicate:
1 copy – retain
1 copy – Demonstration Area

Prepared by __Laura V. Moore__

Reviewed by_____

Librarian Laura Moore crossed out the Black borrower registration section on this monthly report for the Forestville Community Library in January 1942. *FCPL Photographic Archive.*

both. All extant forms from 1942 and 1943 were answered as "white" only. Grids designated for "Negro Borrower Registration" statistics were left blank or crossed out on every monthly record for the Forestville (Great Falls), Falls Church, Herndon, Lorton and McLean Community Libraries.

Surviving FCPL records provide no clues as to why service to Black residents was discontinued in the early 1940s. Simultaneously, FCPL was struggling in 1941 with financial problems, staff resignations and wartime demands. By 1942, WPA assistance was entirely withdrawn, and the county became responsible for operating the library. However, throughout these struggles, FCPL continued to establish new bookmobile stops and expand library access in white communities.[75]

It is possible that FCPL deemed the Fairfax and Falls Church "Colored" stations as having low circulation, which may have led to their closures. FCPL began recording library statistics in November 1940, including records of book stock, circulation, borrower registration, bookmobile service and operational costs. When service began for the county's Black residents at the Fairfax "Colored" Station in January 1941, statistics were kept for the registrants and type of books circulated to the Black community. These statistics were maintained for less than a year, ending in October 1941. For subsequent monthly reports in 1942, designated columns for those statistics were left blank, and white statistics were written over them. Within that ten-month period, 1,179 white residents registered for a library card, while only 46 Black residents became new registrants.

Beginning in 1944, the Extension Division of the Virginia State Library designated a "Service to Negroes" column in its annually published *Statistics of Virginia Public Libraries*. For its 1944–45 and 1945–46 reports, a checkmark indicated whether a system's main library or its branches served the Black community. The county librarian was responsible for completing the Extension Division's annual survey. In the 1944–45 report, Margaret Edwards reported that FCPL did not provide service to Black citizens.[76] However, in the 1945–46 report, newly appointed county librarian Ruth Ashburn stated that the main branch did provide such service.[77]

Subsequent Virginia State Library reports no longer designated a column for "Service to Negroes," presumably because of the new law passed as chapter 170 of the 1946 Acts of Assembly, which required libraries that received state aid to serve all residents. That law, which still appears in the Code of Virginia today under §42.1-55, reads, "The service of books in library systems and libraries receiving state aid shall be free and shall be made available to all persons living in the county, region or municipality."[78] Due to the vagueness of the law's language, many libraries in the commonwealth could still get away with segregating their library services.

FCPL incorporated that inclusive language in a flyer advertising service after ceremoniously launching a new, larger bookmobile in July 1948: "Anyone living or working in Fairfax County is entitled to the free use of all county library services."[79] If FCPL reestablished deposit stations or bookmobile stops in Black communities, it is not apparent in extant records.

FCPL Acquires Books by Black Authors

In May 1945, County Librarian Margaret Edwards wrote to the Extension Division of the state library requesting a list of books by Black authors. On June 1, 1945, Ernestine Grafton, the head of the Extension Division, provided her with a bibliography of Black literature compiled by Mollie Huston Lee.[80] Lee was the first Black librarian in Wake County, North Carolina, and founded the Richard B. Harrison Public Library in Raleigh. It was the first library in that city to serve the Black population when it opened in November 1935.

The Washington YMCA Twelfth Streeters won the 1909–10 Colored Basketball World Championship. Edwin B. Henderson, seen here holding the basketball, moved to Falls Church in 1911 and wrote *The Negro in Sports*. He later helped establish the Fairfax County branch of the NAACP. *FCPL Photographic Archive.*

Evidently, Edwards acquired books from Lee's list, because the June 16, 1945 issue of the *Fairfax Journal* featured the headline "Fairfax Library Has Four Books on Negroes." One of those books was *The Negro in Sports*, by Edwin B. Henderson, a Falls Church resident who founded the NAACP's Fairfax County chapter in 1918. Henderson's book was the first written history of Black athletics. The *Fairfax Journal* article went on to encourage Fairfax County readers to become more familiar with the struggles of Black Americans through reading.[81]

FCPL's Collaboration with Fairfax County Public Schools

When the library system was established in 1939, Fairfax County Public Schools (FCPS), like the rest of Virginia's school districts, maintained a segregated school system. The Public Free Schools Act, passed in 1870, stipulated that school districts in the state were to be separated by race. FCPS did not offer high school education until 1907, at which time, it was only available to white children. At their own expense, Black students had to travel to Manassas or Washington, D.C., to attend high school until 1954, when FCPS finally opened the segregated Luther Jackson High School.

There were sixteen "Colored" elementary schools in operation during the 1939–40 school year, when FCPL was created. Fifteen of those schools had some sort of classroom library, although they were by no means created or maintained equally. One school, Woodlawn, had only 2 books in its entire library. Others had dictionaries, encyclopedias and additional books. Bailey's School had one of the largest libraries during the 1939–40 school year, with 245 books in each of its two classrooms.[82]

Black school libraries were assembled in a variety of ways. Sometimes, FCPS provided tattered and worn books that had formerly been used by white students. School board minutes record that, occasionally, FCPS acquired "Rosenwald Library Units" for Black schools. Mostly, though, it was parent-teacher associations, school leagues, clubs and parents who donated books to the schools. Local Black communities or schools would host parties, luncheons, rallies and carnivals to raise funds for needed supplies.

As early as 1929, the newly established Fairfax County Colored Citizens Association staged a "Citizens' Rally Day" at the "Colored" fairgrounds to raise funds for the establishment of libraries in the Black schools.[83] Representative Oscar DePriest of Illinois, a civil rights activist and the first

Students use the school library at Luther Jackson High School in 1956. When it opened in 1954, it was Fairfax County's first and only high school built for Black students. *FCPL Photographic Archive.*

Black man elected to Congress in the twentieth century, gave a keynote speech at the event. Another organization, the Fairfax Colored School League, gifted its school a sixty-dollar library unit a decade later in December 1940.[84]

In many instances, the teachers raised money and, in some cases, used their own cash to acquire books and other materials for their classrooms. During the 1944–45 school year, Mildred Jennings, a teacher at the Falls Church Colored School, received $19.41 from her class and used it to purchase books, tacks and posters.[85] In that same school year, Annie M. Moore improved the Odricks School library with $15.19 she had received from fundraisers.[86] Historical FCPS school reports document multiple instances of private purchases of books that should have been supplied by county funds.

When the library board of trustees agreed to offer service to Black patrons in July 1940, it also agreed that schools should be served and become book depositories through an agreement with FCPS.[87] One month later, the Fairfax County School Board invited C.W. Dickinson Jr., the director of school libraries and textbooks for the State Department of Education, to discuss potential relations between the Fairfax County School Board and the library board of trustees. At the August 20, 1940 school board meeting, Dickinson suggested that they appoint a committee to prepare a contract between the two boards regarding the handling and distribution of library books among schools. The school board directed Dickinson to prepare the agreement.[88]

On October 1, 1940, library board trustee and superintendent of schools Wilbert T. Woodson presented Dickinson's submitted proposed agreement to the school board. The memorandum stipulated that FCPL would house a collection of public school library books purchased by the school board for circulation to public school children and adults. It further specified that "all state and county public school book funds appropriated for countywide library service shall be used for the purchase of books and other materials needed in the general public education program for adults and children of both races."[89]

The books were to be circulated at regular intervals during the school term and through countywide loan stations during the summer. Books for adult readers were to be circulated from existing library deposit stations, which included public school buildings during the school term. In return, the school board agreed to furnish the library supplies needed to maintain the school library book collection. The school board approved the agreement and revised it again on March 13, 1943.[90] Despite revisions, the agreement always stipulated that books were to be purchased for both races.

Evidence indicates that Black schools did not receive the school board–purchased book units or the same type of service given to the white schools during the 1940s. FCPL's 1945–46 annual report notes, "The regular deposit of twenty-five books (recreational type) to each of sixteen elementary white schools in the county was changed this year to a deposit of forty books every other month."[91] Surviving FCPL circulation reports for school libraries from 1945 to 1949 contain only a single instance of a deposit being made at a Black school. On May 13, 1948, Principal B. Oswald Robinson signed off on a report that said eighty books were circulated at Louise Archer (Vienna Colored) Elementary School.[92]

Despite this lack of support in the 1940s, local Black communities persevered. In September 1946, a branch library for the use of adults opened at the Vienna Colored School (renamed Louise Archer Elementary School in April 1948). Its creation was spearheaded by a surprising ally: two members of the white-only Vienna Library Association, Edna Moody and its president Esther W. Hall. The duo organized the library's creation and

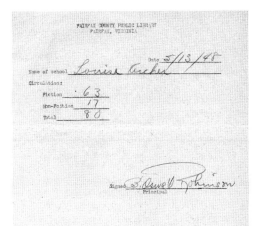

Left: This May 1948 circulation record signed by Louise Archer Elementary School principal B. Oswald Robinson is the only known FCPL book deposit provided to a Black public school during the 1940s. *FCPL Photographic Archive.*

Below: The Vienna Colored School's seventh-grade class pose in 1946. That same year, this building housed a library for Black adults. *Gloria Carter.*

even personally gifted books to get it started.[93] Meanwhile, the Vienna Town Library continued to adhere to its white-only policy.

FCPL also helped establish a Bailey's Crossroads library specifically for the community's Black residents. In 1946, the library board appointed Ruth Ashburn as the new county librarian. Ashburn had formerly served as a librarian for the segregated Purcellville Library. During the summer of

In 1947, the Bailey's Colored School offered library services to the Black community through FCPL's sponsorship. *FCPL Photographic Archive.*

1947, Ashburn, in conjunction with Vivian Frye, the director of the Bailey's Crossroads Summer Playground, and the Fairfax County Recreation Association, sponsored a public library at the Bailey's Colored School. School officials agreed to have the facility open for public library service throughout the academic year. A door-knocking campaign resulted in the addition of more than one hundred books to the library's collection, and Ashburn promised to loan additional FCPL books if circulation justified it. The County Recreation Association agreed to provide a volunteer librarian for at least one evening each week.[94]

By the early 1950s, FCPL bookmobiles were making scheduled stops at segregated schools. In 1951, Mary E. Elliott, a student at the Drexel Institute of Technology School of Library Science in Philadelphia, studied FCPL as a part of her master in library science degree. Her thesis, "The Development of Library Service in Fairfax County, Virginia Since 1939," contains an appendix of FCPL's 1951 schedule of bookmobile routes, which included stops at thirty-two elementary and eight private schools. Each school, including four segregated schools, received a deposit of forty books.[95] Merrifield Elementary was on the Tremont Gardens Route and was visited on the first Tuesday of each month. The bookmobile stopped at Louise Archer Elementary on the second Friday of each month while traveling on the Vienna Route. A second bookmobile visited Fairfax Elementary and Cub Run Elementary on the Burke Route also on the second Friday of each

Helen E. Johnson, a reading helping teacher, works with students in the Luther Jackson High School library in November 1958. *FCPL Photographic Archive.*

month.[96] It is unknown if other Black schools were added to the bookmobile routes prior to the school system's complete desegregation in 1966.

In the mid-1930s, FCPS received grant funding from the federal government's Public Works Administration to build modernized "brick and mortar" white elementary and high schools. These schools included rooms designated for libraries. In 1947, James Lee Elementary School in Falls Church was the first modern all-Black school of this type to have a designated library. Louise Archer Elementary School did not have a standalone library until 1952, when it received an addition.[97] FCPS constructed five additional all-Black schools with designated libraries between 1952 and 1956: Drew-Smith (1952), Oak Grove (1952), Eleven Oaks (1953), Luther Jackson High School (1954) and Lillian Carey (1956).

In 1960, FCPS slowly began admitting Black students to white schools. Under mounting legal pressure, FCPS drafted a plan to accelerate the process.

Mabel Jolly, seen here in 1959, was the school librarian for Luther Jackson High School's entire operation from 1954 to 1966. *FCPL Photographic Archive.*

By then, all FCPL library facilities were already open to everyone. How was it possible that the public libraries in Fairfax County were desegregated but public schools were not, especially since the Superintendent of Schools Wilbert T. Woodson was also on the library board of trustees?

Woodson's personal beliefs, shared by many others at the time, were that libraries were less intimate environments than schools and thus more conducive to integration. On July 6, 1959, he wrote to school board member Robert F. Davis:

> *The order to desegregate schools is highly improper and infringes on human rights. To force integration of schools is to force social mixing, since attendance in public schools is usually compulsory. Next to the home, the*

public school brings people into closest social relationship. Association in hotels, restaurants, buses, trains, airplanes and churches is less serious, since relationships among people in these situations is not so close or intimate and people have a choice with whom they wish to associate, it not being required by law, as pupils in a classroom and in school activities.[98]

Wilbert Tucker Woodson was the Superintendent of Fairfax County Public Schools from 1929 to 1961. He helped direct the policy of FCPL as a member of the library board of trustees from 1939 to 1961. *FCPL Photographic Archive.*

Although Woodson personally opposed school integration, the decision to desegregate FCPS was not his to make; rather, it was the school board's. Even after Woodson's retirement from FCPS—and, by default, the library board—in 1961, it took another five years for FCPS to fully integrate.

Immediately following the Supreme Court's *Brown v. Board of Education* decision, which declared school segregation unconstitutional, Virginia's state government embarked on a policy known as "Massive Resistance." Led by Senator Harry F. Byrd Sr. and his political machine known as the Byrd Organization, the commonwealth fiercely opposed the integration of public schools, passing anti-desegregation legislation known as the Stanley Plan in 1956. The plan contained a series of laws that allowed the governor to shut down any school that did integrate and created a State Pupil Placement Board that blocked Black students from being assigned to white schools. Even after state and federal lawsuits overruled "Massive Resistance" policies, school desegregation in the commonwealth continued to move at a glacial pace. The seven segregated Black schools in Fairfax County were either closed or fully integrated between 1964 and 1966.

FCPL EXPANDS AND OPENS BRANCHES

From 1939 to 1950, FCPL provided service only by bookmobile.[99] The first library building in Fairfax was initially used for housing only the book collection, bookmobile and staff. By 1947, the collection had grown so much that Chairman John Bethune asked the Fairfax County Board of Supervisors for an addition. The board agreed, and construction began two years later.[100] The book collection expanded into the garage, and the building received a

The reception dedicating the expanded Headquarters Library on February 13, 1950: *Seated from left to right*: Ruth Ashburn, librarian; Captain John F. Bethune, chairman of the library board; and Mrs. Fred Robinson, library board. *Standing from left to right*: William J. Duvall, contractor; Wilbert T. Woodson, library board and superintendent of schools; Earl B. Bailey, architect; William L. Carne, library board; and Harry Davis, contractor. *FCPL Photographic Archive.*

twenty-three-by-twenty-three-foot rear addition and an eighteen-by-forty-four-foot attached garage for the bookmobile.

Upon these additions' completion in February 1950, the library tripled in size but contained only one table with four chairs to be shared by patrons and library staff.[101] Two stools were designated for children. There is no surviving documentation indicating whether Black residents could use the library when it opened, nor do any longtime Fairfax County residents interviewed remember.

Two years later, on July 14, 1952, the library board of trustees asked the Extension Division of the Virginia State Library to conduct a survey of the conditions of FCPL. The resulting report, published in November 1952 by Christine Coffey, the assistant Extension Division librarian, was mostly negative. Coffey found that FCPL suffered from an inadequate collection, insufficient financial support, the lack of a complete catalogue, the neglect in service to adults, poorly chosen bookmobile stops, a deficiency in personnel and overall poor service.

Coffey began her report with a quote from Amy Winslow of the American Library Association: "The public library provides, on equal terms, free service to all individuals and groups in the community."[102] She made no mention of whether FCPL provided service to Black residents. She did, however, recommend that "the Headquarters Library should be opened to all residents of the county wherever they live. Indeed, failure to do so is a violation of one of the requirements made by the state library board of public libraries receiving state aid."[103]

An earlier May 1952 memo to the library board of trustees from its budget committee reiterated: "It is the general purpose of the library board to maintain and to extend to *all* freeholders and residents of Fairfax County library services commensurate with the need of and demand for such services."[104]

Following the release of the state's scathing 1952 report, the library board of trustees appointed Mary K. McCulloch as Fairfax County library director on July 13, 1953, and it tasked her with reorganizing FCPL. After less than two weeks on the job, on July 27, 1953, McCulloch closed the library to the public for six months for a complete inventorying, reorganization and remodeling. The bookmobile garage was converted into office space with expanded library shelving, a card catalogue was created and preparations were made to open two new branches. After the remodeling and reorganization, the Headquarters Library reopened on December 21, 1953, and bookmobile service resumed on January 4, 1954.[105]

On that same date in 1954, FCPL's first branch, Thomas Jefferson, opened to the public in Falls Church, followed by the Martha Washington branch in Alexandria on May 2. Community efforts to open FCPL branches had been brewing since 1952. Several citizens' groups had earlier organized to petition the Fairfax County Board of Supervisors and the library board of trustees for branch service. The library board allowed these "Friends of the Library" groups to raise funds for establishing branches, locate potential quarters, provide equipment and enlist volunteer help to start branches.

At the August 17, 1953 library board of trustees meeting, trustee Kathryn Robinson motioned that communities be permitted to suggest names for their branches. FCPS superintendent and trustee Wilbert T. Woodson added on to the motion that the library board set the policy that all future branches be named for famous deceased Virginians. The board passed the motion, and the policy remained in place until 1983.[106] As of 2022, eight of FCPL's twenty-three branches retain the names of famous Virginians, all of whom are white.

When FCPL's first branch, Thomas Jefferson, opened in the rear of the Family Barber Shop in the Graham Road Shopping Center in Falls Church,

Mary K. McCulloch was the director of FCPL from 1953 to 1969. *FCPL Photographic Archive.*

the Friends of the Thomas Jefferson Library created flyers promoting its open house on January 9, inviting "everybody" and offering "a card for everyone who can print his own name."[107] After the opening, a fundraising flyer issued by the Friends declared the branch "open, free of charge to all residents of the area."[108] The *Fairfax County Sun Echo* also confirmed the library's inclusiveness in a May 14, 1954 article, saying, "It may be used by all county residents, free of charge."[109]

Although the library had its own private entrance at the back of the white-owned barbershop, it is unclear whether Black residents would have felt comfortable using it—or if it was accessed by the Black community during its year of operation in that storefront. The Thomas Jefferson branch quickly outgrew the barbershop space and moved into a two-bedroom apartment in Jefferson Village Apartments. It later reopened in new quarters in November 1962, becoming FCPL's first permanent branch library located in a building constructed by Fairfax County specifically for this use.[110]

After the Martha Washington branch's opening in May 1954, a third branch, George Mason, opened in Annandale in February 1955, followed by Dolley Madison in McLean in December 1956, Richard Byrd in Springfield in January 1958 and Woodrow Wilson in Falls Church in January 1961. No documentation exists of FCPL's integration policies when opening these branches.

In 1955, the library board of trustees outlined its purpose in a report: "It is the function of the library board to give policy guidance to the director

IT'S OPEN!

The Thomas Jefferson Library, Branch of the Fairfax County Library is now open.

Hours: Monday, Wednesday, Friday 1-5 and 7 - 9. Saturday 9 - 1.

Place: 1528 Arlington Blvd. - Rear of the Family Barber Shop in the Graham Road
         Shopping Center, with its own entrance in the rear of the shopping center.

Books: Any number per card. A card for everyone who can print his own name.

Open House - Saturday, January 9 from 1 to 2 PM. Everybody invited.

The Friends of the Thomas Jefferson Library invited everyone to the new branch's open house on January 9, 1954. *FCPL Photographic Archive.*

in order that library service may be made freely available to ALL citizens of Fairfax County."[111] That same year, FCPL added a new deposit station in a Black residence in Chantilly.[112] A *Washington Sunday Star* article from February 24, 1957, is the earliest recorded statement specifying that FCPL was open to both white and Black residents. "Spokesmen for libraries in the nearby Virginia area said library facilities are open to colored residents in Fairfax and Arlington Counties and cities of Alexandria and Falls Church," reported correspondent Tom Burke during his coverage of Purcellville Library's integration suit.[113]

Despite FCPL appearing to be open to everyone in the 1950s, it did not effectively relay this message to Black residents. Library student Bernice Lloyd Bell confirmed this in her August 1963 thesis, "Integration in Public Library Service in Thirteen Southern States, 1954–1962," noting that FCPL never made any special efforts to notify the county's Black residents of available library services.[114]

In May 2021, FCPL's Virginia Room staff asked several longtime Black residents whether they used FCPL facilities while growing up in the 1950s. Everyone interviewed said they never went to the library, nor did they remember the bookmobile visiting their neighborhood. "My library experience was through our schools," recalled one resident.[115] Those interviewed did not specifically recall whether FCPL was ever segregated in the 1950s. Black residents likely did not feel welcome visiting libraries while other public accommodations in the county, such as restaurants, motels, hospitals and even the public schools themselves, remained segregated. However, several Vienna residents who were interviewed still remembered not being allowed into the Vienna Town Library and recall the community efforts to recruit FCPL's help to change this.

ESTABLISHING THE PATRICK HENRY LIBRARY BRANCH

While the previous five FCPL branches and main library were integrated when they were opened between 1953 and 1961, Patrick Henry Library was the first branch established with the explicit purpose of being accessible to all residents of the town of Vienna. Until its opening in 1962, Vienna's Black residents were excluded from the only library around, the Vienna Town Library.

Some members of the Vienna Library Association did not agree with this policy and were concerned that the town's Black citizens, particularly Black children, did not have library access. In early 1946, a few members donated books and helped create a branch library for adults in the Vienna Colored School.[116] That June, the Vienna Library Association voted to present duplicate books to the school's principal Louise Archer for use by the school's children.[117]

On January 24, 1946, volunteer librarian June Waldrip wrote to Ernestine Grafton, the head of the Extension Division of the state library, describing some of these efforts:

> *It is too bad we have no library for negroes. This library was chartered in 1913 for "the white people of Vienna"—hence I cannot serve books to*

Patrick Henry Library was housed in this storefront in the Vienna Shopping Center from 1962 to 1971. *FCPL Photographic Archive.*

colored folk. But the President Mrs. [Esther W.] *Hall and myself—and a few others interested have contributed small amounts of money—books—to the few shelves of books Mrs.* [Louise] *Archer, the principal, has in her school (the colored school)."*[118]

The Vienna Library Association always held itself aloof from FCPL and refused to abide by the library board's policies and requirements in order to receive bookmobile service as a community library. It later resisted pressure to assimilate into an FCPL branch. The community's frustration with the association reached a climax in the 1950s due to an incident with the Carter family.

William McKinley Carter (1897–1977), a prominent Black citizen of Vienna, was a retired Internal Revenue Service employee and descendant of the Carter family that had lived in neighboring Freedom Hill since 1842.[119] He was a charter member of the Fairfax County branch of the NAACP and the longtime president of the Citizens Progressive Association of Vienna.[120] At some point in the 1950s, a white woman checked out books from the Vienna Town Library for Carter's children. Wyndell Carter, one of those children, later recalled, "Once the board of trustees found out we had books; they came and took them back. That kind of perturbed my dad and some friends."[121]

Another of Carter's children, Maurice Carter (1924–2010), who was active in civic affairs, attended a Vienna Town Council meeting on June 6, 1955, seeking support for the Vienna Lions Little-League. During the meeting, the Vienna Library Association asked the council for its annual contribution to the Vienna Town Library. Based on recollections from twenty years later, Carter stood up and objected to the donation, demanding that the association change its library charter to serve all Vienna residents.[122] The Vienna Town Council approved the contribution anyway.[123]

In 1958, disgruntled citizens met in William Carter's living room and informally established the "Friends of the Library Vienna, Virginia," a biracial organization. Kenton Kilmer, the son of poet Joyce Kilmer, was informally made chairman and wrote to Florence Yoder, the head of the Extension Division of the Virginia State Library, requesting that a survey be conducted regarding library service in the town of Vienna.[124] Yoder recommended he contact FCPL to make arrangements for branch service instead.[125]

Elsa Burrowes, Patrick Henry Library's branch manager from 1970 to 1982, was hired by FCPL as Patrick Henry's reference librarian in 1968. Her orientation included a briefing on the formation of that branch. She

Right: William McKinley Carter, a civil rights activist, fought to make library services available to everyone in the Town of Vienna. *FCPL Photographic Archive.*

Below: In October 1958, Maurice Carter introduced a resolution to permit all Vienna citizens to use the town's library facilities. *FCPL Photographic Archive.*

recalled in May 2021: "The Friends [were] determined to bring a branch of Fairfax County Public Library to Vienna, because in the late 1950s to early 1960s, at least, it was understood that Fairfax County Public Library served 'everybody.'"[126]

Before courting FCPL, the Friends attempted to work with the existing Vienna Library Association. They invited Paul Stenger, the president of the association, to their charter meeting on October 14, 1958. At the meeting, the Vienna Friends defined their goals, appointed committees, adopted resolutions and named Kenton Kilmer the group's temporary group chairman until an official election could be carried out in January 1959.[127] Carter's son Maurice introduced a resolution to have the Vienna Library Association's charter changed to "permit all citizens of Vienna use of the library facilities" if the town library was to continue operating in its present location.[128] At the time, the legal ownership of the Vienna Town Library's property on Center Street and Maple Avenue was in question.

Paul Stenger objected, calling the motion premature, but the Friends ignored him and passed it.[129] "They know we're trying to clear title to the land and want to develop the library. They said they were going to organize to help us. They talked to me, and I went to their first meeting. Then they passed the resolution. They don't appear to be a friend," said Stenger.[130] Interviewed after the meeting by a *Northern Virginia Sun* reporter, Stenger could not remember any Black residents ever entering the library to borrow books. However, he did say the library loaned books out to "Colored groups" and Louise Archer Elementary School.[131]

Four months later, the Friends formally organized in February 1959, with a membership of ninety individuals.[132] The officers elected were Kenton Kilmer, president; David Mayer, vice-president; Katherine Brand, corresponding secretary; Ross Netherton, record secretary; and William Carter, treasurer.[133] "By electing Carter, we were saying that this organization was going to be for all people of Vienna, and McKinley handled himself and the Friends' finances in an exemplary manner," recalled Ross Netherton's wife, Nan, in 1990.[134]

Ross Netherton and Katherine Brand met with FCPL Director Mary McCulloch on January 7, 1959, to discuss establishing a branch in town.[135] Netherton later recalled in 1970 that "Mrs. McCulloch had been extremely helpful in working to get a branch library established in Vienna."[136] Later that month, on January 21, 1959, Kilmer, Carter, Brand, Netherton and a couple of other Vienna citizens accompanied Director McCulloch on a tour of the George Mason and Richard Byrd branches to get an idea of what branch service would entail.[137]

The Friends met with the library board of trustees in late 1959, and it was decided that if the Friends' membership agreed to the board's policies and requirements for establishing a new branch by November, money could be reserved for it in the 1961 county budget.[138] Director McCulloch attended the Friends' October 30, 1959 meeting, and its members agreed to move forward with establishing an FCPL branch in Vienna.[139] Unfortunately, the county executive made significant cuts to the 1961 library budget, which eliminated the proposed Vienna branch that year.[140] Undaunted, the Friends persevered.

One of the requirements to establish the branch was to raise 25 percent of the library's first year of operating expenses, a cost of $7,500. The remaining balance would be assumed by Fairfax County, including all operational costs after its first year of opening. Consequently, the Friends embarked on an aggressive fundraising campaign for the library in the summer of 1960.

By September 1960, the Friends' membership had exploded to 1,800 individuals.[141] Local Vienna organizations and businesses, including the Vienna Women's Club, Vienna Optimists, Five Hills Garden Club, Young Ladies Domestic Club, Welcome Wagon Club, Vienna Trust Co. and the Ayr Hill subdivision, donated to the effort. Jimmy Mallis of the Rollin Road Restaurant created his own fundraiser by donating all proceeds from the cups of coffee purchased at his restaurant.[142] One of the biggest donors was Stephens G. Yeonas, a Vienna developer who donated $2,500 in September 1960.[143]

Left to right: Vienna mayor Guy M. Wilson looks on as Friends president Kenton Kilmer receives a $2,500 check from developer Stephen G. Yeonas in September 1960. *FCPL Photographic Archive.*

The Vienna Town Council, which had supported the white-only Vienna Town Library with financial contributions for nearly half a century, enthusiastically supported the efforts to bring an FCPL branch to the town. In the fall of 1960, the council passed a resolution pledging financial support if the Friends' efforts fell short. The council's assistance went unneeded, as the Friends surpassed their financial goal, netting $9,050.50 by the November 1960 deadline.[144] Because of their successful fundraising efforts, the Fairfax County Board of Supervisors agreed to provide funds for opening a branch in the 1962 budget in December 1960.[145] Library trustee Nan Watters moved that the branch be named for Patrick Henry, and it was approved by the library board at its March 13, 1961 meeting.[146]

The library board also approved renting space in the Vienna Shopping Center at 325 Maple Avenue East for the Patrick Henry Library and signed a five-year $525 monthly lease on January 8, 1962.[147] Later that month, Director McCulloch completed signing the lease in the unfinished library space, with the Friends, including William Carter, in attendance. The Friends, in turn, gave her an $8,800 check made out to the county for the required 25 percent first year's operating expenses. They reserved the remaining funds for a gala on the library's opening day and other overhead expenses.

The Friends held an open house at Patrick Henry Library on Sunday, April 8, 1962. Invitations to the public noted the event was "open to all Vienna residents."[148] Over 1,500 patrons attended, including Vienna councilmen and members of the Fairfax County Board of Supervisors.[149] The library officially opened the following morning at 10:00 a.m., with Helen Walker as the branch manager overseeing a collection of 6,200 books. The first day saw 367 customers check out books.[150] By the end of the first three weeks, Patrick Henry had registered 1,359 borrowers.[151]

At a ceremony on November 17, 1968, a special bookshelf was dedicated to William and Lillian Carter. The Friends of the Library had suggested the idea for the honorary shelf as a designated space for gifted books presented to the library. The first gift to be featured was the *International Encyclopedia of Negro Life and History*. Members of the Carter family, library staff, FCPL Director Mary McCulloch, Vienna Mayor James Martinelli and Centreville District Supervisor Martha Pennino attended the ceremony.[152]

The opening of the Patrick Henry branch decimated the Vienna Town Library. "There was a lot of ill feelings with the start of the other library," recalled Jean Rockwell, a former member of the Vienna Library Association, in 1990.[153] By November 1962, Mary McCulloch reported to Florence Yoder, the head of the Extension Division at the Virginia State Library,

Patrons hold up a poster, which says, "Everyone Welcome," in front of the Patrick Henry Library, promoting its April 1962 open house. *FCPL Photographic Archive.*

Friends president Ross Netherton with William McKinley Carter and his sister-in-law Somerville Monroe at the dedication of the Carter Shelf in Patrick Henry Library on November 17, 1968. *FCPL Photographic Archive.*

William McKinley Carter (*center*) attends the dedication of the new Patrick Henry Library on September 5, 1971. *FCPL Photographic Archive.*

that the library was open only eight or nine hours a week and had very little business.[154] Despite this, the Vienna Library Association still wanted to start a building campaign for its own new library. The association had been sporadically receiving donations for a new building since the 1950s, including funds raised by a minstrel show benefit that was staged by the Vienna Lions Club and sponsored by the Vienna Hills Women's Club in November 1956.[155] However, the construction of a new library never became reality.

In 1969, the dispute over the legal ownership of the land underneath the original Vienna Town Library was settled, and the county exchanged properties to pave the way for a permanent Patrick Henry Library building. The original Vienna Town Library was moved next to the Freeman Store on Mill Street, and a permanent Patrick Henry Library was constructed there, opening on September 7, 1971.

THE FIRST BLACK EMPLOYEE AT FCPL

Dora Lee (Anderson) Johnson (1920–1999) is the earliest known Black employee of FCPL. Johnson was the great-granddaughter of Frank Napper, a freed enslaved person. Napper was one of the earliest settlers of Bowmantown, a historically Black village in Loudoun County, Virginia, established shortly before the Civil War.[156] Johnson was born in Aldie, Virginia, on January 10, 1920, and received only a third-grade education.[157]

Early library personnel records no longer exist, making it difficult to determine when Johnson was hired; however, her name first appears on a 1957 roster of library employee salaries, listing her as a Custodian I at the Thomas Jefferson branch.[158] She also appears in the oldest existing FCPL staff directory, dated July 1962. Johnson, who resided in Leesburg

Dora Lee Johnson working in the new Headquarters Library in 1963. *FCPL Photographic Archive.*

at the time, is listed as working in the Maintenance Department and General Delivery at Thomas Jefferson.[159] She also did book mending at the new Headquarters Library in Fairfax, which opened in 1962. Johnson later moved to Falls Church and remained on the maintenance staff at Headquarters until mid-1968. She went on to work for Fairfax County Public Schools as a cafeteria worker. After her husband died, Johnson remarried in 1980 and went by Dora Lee Morgan. She passed away in Alexandria on February 23, 1999.[160]

The First Black Library Professionals at FCPL

At the library board of trustees meeting on September 9, 1963, the minutes recorded the following:

> *The Fairfax County Public Library has recently employed a well-qualified library aide who is a negro; she has been assigned to the Thomas Jefferson branch, and it is understood that she is well received by staff and patrons. A negro library page has also been employed at the Headquarters Library.*[161]

This library aide was twenty-three-year-old Janice Juanita Bragg (1938–2020) of McLean, Virginia. Bragg left FCPL by October 1964 and went on to become a teacher for the Washington, D.C. and Baltimore City Public School Systems.[162] Bragg passed away on May 16, 2020, in Elkridge, Maryland.[163] The unnamed library page mentioned in the minutes as being employed at the Headquarters Library has not yet been identified.

Norma Jean Lyles (1941–2019), a 1959 graduate of Luther Jackson High School, was another early Black employee of FCPL. Born in Washington, D.C., she grew up in Falls Church. While at Luther Jackson, she participated in many extracurricular activities, including safety patrol, majorettes, choir and the girls' basketball team.[164] Hired as a newlywed by FCPL between 1965 and 1966, Lyles worked in the Central Registration and Overdues Department at the Headquarters Library until 1968.

Nearly twenty years later, in 1989, Nan Netherton conducted a sixty-minute oral history interview with retired library director Mary K. McCulloch about her experiences at FCPL. McCulloch discussed a variety of topics concerning her career as director from 1953 to 1969. Netherton asked her about employee discrimination:

Norma Jean Lyles was a majorette at Luther Jackson High School in 1958. She went on to work in the Central Registration and Overdues Department at the Headquarters Library around 1965. *FCPL Photographic Archive.*

Netherton: What about discrimination?…Did you and your personnel and the Library Board of Trustees address this problem of people in minorities who might come and seek a job in the library system in Fairfax County?

McCulloch: I never had any problem in that area whatsoever.

Netherton: Well, I was just wondering if you remembered applications from Black candidates?

McCulloch: I remember it was difficult to find professional Black librarians if you were looking for some.[165]

The First Black Library Trustee of FCPL

At the library board of trustees meeting on September 19, 1973, Vera P. Swann of Springfield District was sworn in as the first Black member of the library board.[166] Vera Peral Poe was born in 1931 in Cheraw, South Carolina, and graduated from Johnson C. Smith University in Charlotte, North Carolina, in 1951.[167] Poe married Reverend Darius L. Swann, PhD (1924–2020), the Presbyterian Church's first Black missionary assigned to

76

a non-African country. The couple spent a decade working as missionaries in India.

In 1964, the Swanns moved to Charlotte, North Carolina, and attempted to send their son, James Swann, to the integrated Seversville School, located two blocks from their house. Their son returned home with a note from the principal notifying his parents that he had to attend the segregated Biddleville School, which was twice as far away, before he could transfer to Seversville. After refusing to do this, the Swanns sued the school system in January 1965 and were represented by civil rights attorney Julius L. Chambers. *Swann v. Charlotte-Mecklenburg Board of Education* went to the Supreme Court in 1971. Their ruling upheld court-ordered busing in the Charlotte-Mecklenburg school district, which paved the way for the use of busing nationally as a means of desegregating schools.[168]

Following the ruling, the Swanns moved to Fairfax County in the early 1970s. Vera Swann served on the library board of trustees for four years until 1977, when she was unavailable for reappointment. Swan went on to teach at the Alexandria campus of Northern Virginia Community College and authored several books on Black Presbyterian history. Her husband, Reverend Darius Swann, passed away on March 8, 2020, but Vera Swann continues to live in Northern Virginia.

FCPL MOVES FORWARD

FCPL's commitment to provide library services to all Fairfax County citizens slowly began in the 1950s and progressed over the next twenty years with the opening of Patrick Henry Library in Vienna and the hiring and appointment of Black library staff and a library board member. Throughout the 1960s, FCPL was one of the forefront county agencies promoting inclusion and engaging with Black communities. By 1969, the system was hosting "Get Acquainted" evening programs with Black families and working with teenagers in Gum Springs, the oldest Black community in the county, to bring better service to them. In October 1972, the library board of trustees reaffirmed its commitment to all Fairfax County citizens, writing in its policy manual: "FCPL serves a diverse population with wide-ranging and ever-increasing needs and interests (expressed and unexpressed) for the information and assistance available in library materials. The library is dedicated to the concept of service to everyone."[169]

The FCPL Bookmobile visits a neighborhood in June 1973. *FCPL Photographic Archive.*

RECOGNITION

On February 7, 1987, Patrick Henry Library rededicated the Carter collection of materials in a festive ceremony. At the end of his speech, Vondell Carter presented the library with a portrait of his parents, William Carter and Lillian Carter, which still greets everyone who uses the library's meeting room.[170] Books from the Carter shelf are now in FCPL's Virginia Room. The Little Library of Vienna, with most of its original books intact, is now a museum.

The name "Little Library of Vienna" was chosen deliberately, leaving out the word "community" to recognize that it was not always accessible to everyone in town. The library currently has an integrated board and is adding information about its history of segregation to its brochures. Historic Vienna Inc., which oversees the library's museum and other historic structures in Vienna, recently hosted a 2022 exhibit called *Vienna's African American Trailblazers*, which included information about the Carter family and their work in achieving library integration.

Existing Sites

The Site of Forestville (Great Falls) Library (1938–1959)
9818 Georgetown Pike, Great Falls, VA 22066

The Forestville Library opened in 1938 and operated out of the Great Falls Grange before moving next door to the Forestville School building in 1959. The library closed in 1961. As a partnering community library with FCPL in the 1940s, it only served white residents. Library shelving that was built to house the book collection can still be found inside the Grange, which is now owned by Fairfax County Park Authority.

The Site of Herndon Fortnightly Club Library (1927–1971)
660 Spring Street, Herndon, VA 20170

In 1927, the Good Templars donated a lot, and the Herndon Fortnightly Club constructed this building as a public library for the town's white citizens. FCPL leased the building in 1971 and opened the Herndon Fortnightly branch on March 7, 1972. It operated here until a new Herndon Fortnightly Library opened on Center Street in May 1995. This building is currently home to the Quaker community's Herndon Friends Meeting.

Huddleson Memorial Library
3999 University Drive, Fairfax, VA 22030

Originally founded as Fairfax County Library in 1930, this white-only library opened two years later. After a series of moves, in 1938, the library permanently moved into Old Town Hall, where it still exists on the second floor. The library was renamed the Town of Fairfax Library after FCPL was created in 1939, and again, in 1962, it was renamed the Huddleson Memorial Library in honor of Nellie H. Huddleson.

The Little Library Museum
164 Mill Street Northeast, Vienna, VA 22180

Built in 1897, the Vienna Town Library was segregated from the beginning. The building has been relocated twice (in 1912 and 1970). The museum is open on the first Sunday of every month, and private tours can be scheduled. The museum maintains the original card catalogue and book collection.

Huddleson Memorial Library is still located on the second floor of Old Town Hall. In the early morning hours of August 14, 2020, one of the building's front columns crashed to the ground. *Authors' photograph.*

The former Vienna Town Library is now the Little Library Museum. *Authors' photograph.*

The original Patrick Henry Library storefront now houses a Popeyes. *Authors' photograph.*

FCPL's first branch, Thomas Jefferson, was located in the back of the Family Barber Shop in the Graham Center. The storefront currently houses a dentist's office. *Authors' photograph.*

Louise Archer Elementary School
324 Nutley Street Northwest, Vienna, VA 22180

In 1946, a branch library for use by Black adults opened in Vienna Colored School, later renamed the Louise Archer Elementary School. Members of the white-only Vienna Library Association helped organize its creation, although the enterprise was short-lived. The segregated school was later serviced by FCPL's bookmobile in the 1950s. Louise Archer was a frame-construction building and was opened in 1939. It has since been bricked over and received several additions.

The Site of Patrick Henry Library (1962–1971)
325 Maple Avenue East, Vienna, VA 22180

Patrick Henry Library was the first branch specifically established to serve all residents of the Town of Vienna. Prior to its opening in 1962, Vienna's Black residents were barred from using the only library around, Vienna Town Library. Patrick Henry operated out of this storefront until it moved into its current building at 101 Maple Avenue East in 1971. The former library space currently houses a Popeyes restaurant.

The Site of Thomas Jefferson Library (1954–1955)
7244 Arlington Boulevard, Falls Church, VA 22042

The first branch of FCPL resided in the rear of Buck Carter's Family Barber Shop. When it was opened on January 4, 1954, it became the first documented instance of a FCPL facility being open to all citizens. The branch operated out of this location, now a dentist's office, for a year.

CITY OF FALLS CHURCH

*A*djacent to Fairfax County is the thriving city of Falls Church. Its namesake, a brick Episcopal church completed in 1769, still stands today at East Fairfax and South Washington Streets. Once part of Fairfax County, Falls Church became a township in 1875 and incorporated as a city in 1948. Right in the center of the city is the recently renovated Mary Riley Styles Public Library, which traces its roots to the nineteenth century.

THE ORIGINS OF FALLS CHURCH PUBLIC LIBRARY

In 1899, the Village Improvement Society of Falls Church established the Falls Church Library. It officially opened in May 1900.[171] George W. Hawxhurst, the mayor of Falls Church and a member of the society, provided the library's inaugural home in a small structure behind his house on Columbia Street. Hawxhurst acted as a librarian, and his daughter Nellie Hawxhurst assisted him.[172] In order to efficiently govern and maintain the enterprise, the Village Improvement Society set up a library association and a board of control to oversee operations.

The Falls Church Library was initially subscription-based, and users were required to pay a one-dollar annual fee or five dollars for a permanent membership. Members could access the library every Tuesday, Thursday and Saturday for three hours. Black residents were undoubtedly barred from using the library from its inception, as the town was strictly segregated.

The original Falls Church Public Library, pictured here in 1903, operated behind George W. Hawxhurst's house from 1900 to 1906. *From the* Washington Times.

The library's collection comprised 407 titles, most of which were contributed by members. The library association's President Pickering Dodge had the authority to purchase new books and encouraged subscribers to send in requests. Within the library's first six months, subscribers checked out books 977 times.[173] By 1903, the collection had grown to 650 titles. That year, businesses from Falls Church and Washington, D.C., sponsored the publication of a *Catalogue of Books*, which featured the titles, authors and call numbers of the library's collection.[174]

In September 1906, Hawxhurst was appointed the town's postmaster and moved the library from his backyard into the back of Falls Church Post Office on Broad Street. The library association continued to oversee its operation and grew its collection to 750 titles before quietly disbanding in 1909. With no one to manage it, the Falls Church Library fell into neglect, and many of the books disappeared from the post office over the years.[175] In 1913, a valiant group of local women came to the library's rescue and formed the Civic League to rejuvenate the failing enterprise. They salvaged what remained of the original collection, boosted it with their own donations and relocated the 500-volume venture into a small nook in the former Congregational Church building at 222 North Washington Street. The issue of cramped quarters and a lack of space plagued the library for the next half-century, forcing numerous relocations.

The Civic League, which renamed itself the Falls Church Woman's Club after joining the Federation of Women's Clubs in 1916, relocated the library again when additional room became available in a new commercial building on Washington Street in East Falls Church. A short time later, it moved a few doors down into a space provided by Dr. M.E. Church at the intersection of Washington Street and Fairfax Drive. At that location, the library operated two afternoons a week and continued to charge one-dollar annual fees for usage. This rate eventually changed to five cents per book each week with a daily two-cent fine for overdue materials.[176]

In 1919, the library moved back into the old Congregational Church building, where it remained for the next thirty years. The Town of Falls Church's school board had just purchased the building and was using it to ease the overcrowded conditions at the all-white Jefferson School. The old church continued to house the school's first three grades until the Madison School opened in 1926. Because classrooms took up much of the building, the library was relegated to a corner of two classrooms and was screened off with chicken wire.[177] Over the next decade, the library arranged a borrowing program with the Jefferson School and, later, the Madison School, circulating recommended books to each class of white students.[178]

During this time, the town did not operate any schools for Black children, as most of Falls Church's Black landowners were no longer living within the town's limits. In 1890, the town council voted to retrocede one-third of its land, where a large Black community lived, back to Fairfax County. The council's objective was to eliminate the Black vote, which had been influencing local elections. The retroceded land was incorporated into Fairfax County's Falls Church Magisterial District, whose school board built a cramped one-room Falls Church Colored School for Black children in 1892. Consequently, it is unlikely that Black residents would have accessed the Falls Church Library in a building used by the town's school board, which exclusively catered to white children. The town's school board later transferred the title of the building to the town council in 1937.[179]

When the Woman's Club Library Committee returned the library to its old quarters in the former church building, it was chaired by Mary Riley Styles. Styles was a tireless advocate for the library and chaired the library committee for decades until ill health forced her to resign shortly before her death in 1946. The running joke in the Styles household was that, for Mary, the library came first, and family came second. Styles was also active in

A scenic 1904 view of Falls Church's Congregational Church. The building was later used as a library, school, gymnasium, police station and town hall. *FCPL Photographic Archive.*

several other Falls Church civic organizations and clubs, including Daughters of the American Revolution, American War Mothers and the Robert E. Lee Chapter of United Daughters of the Confederacy. Styles and the library committee directed policymaking for the library; however, records do not survive indicating their attitudes toward serving Black residents.

Mary Riley Styles chaired the Falls Church Woman's Club Library Committee for nearly thirty years. Falls Church Public Library was renamed in her honor in 1977. *Mary Riley Styles Public Library, Local History Collection, Falls Church, VA.*

In 1928, the Town of Falls Church passed an ordinance formally establishing the Falls Church Public Library and agreed to financially support the Woman's Club Library Committee with an annual stipend of $300. "Three hundred dollars was the first amount the city ever appropriated for the library. The way my mother acted, you would have thought it was $3,000," recalled Mary Riley Styles's daughter Elizabeth Styles in 1958.[180] The town's annual appropriation and continued revenue from subscription fees barely sustained the growing Falls Church Library over the next decade. By 1939, Falls Church Library had grown too unwieldy for the women to manage. Consequently, they decided to gift the library to the town so that it could be better funded and more efficiently serve the community. The town agreed to have the woman's club continue to run the library, an arrangement that lasted for a decade.

During that same year, the Fairfax County Board of Supervisors established the Fairfax County Public Library (FCPL) system. The Falls Church Library, in addition to the Forestville, Herndon, Fairfax and McLean community libraries, agreed to support and participate in the new initiative. They all approved loaning books from their collection for circulation through the county's free library system. In return, each participating community library received books deposited by the FCPL Bookmobile.

When FCPL agreed to serve Fairfax County's Black residents at a library board meeting on July 22, 1940, it noted, "None of the books from the various community libraries will be available for negro service."[181] Beyond being segregated, Falls Church Library completely barred the town's Black residents from using its services. Despite this, FCPL did set up a "Colored" bookmobile deposit station in Falls Church in January 1941; however, its exact location remains unknown, and it was discontinued by 1945.

During the same month of the opening of the Falls Church "Colored" deposit station, Annie Margaret Lester, who was employed as the first paid librarian in 1931, announced that Falls Church Library was now officially

In December 1941, Falls Church librarian Anna Margaret Lester completed this monthly record form for the partnering Fairfax County Public Library. The Falls Church Library served only the town's white residents at that time. *FCPL Photographic Archive.*

operating on a free basis, with increased services in larger quarters. The town council had since purchased the old Congregational Church building for use as a town hall and designated a new space within it for the library. The library's hours increased to include five days a week, with books from the FCPL Bookmobile being loaned for two-month periods to further supplement the library's own growing book collection.[182]

Although library services were now freely available to white Falls Church residents, the library remained inaccessible to Black residents. Surviving FCPL monthly records of circulation, registration and book stock for partnering community libraries confirm this policy. The monthly record form had a prompt that asked whether service was provided to white residents, Black residents or both. All extant forms from 1942 and 1943 were answered with "white" only. Designated spaces for "Negro Borrower Registration" statistics were left blank on every monthly record form for the Falls Church Library during those years.

The following year, the Extension Division of the Virginia State Library designated a "Service to Negroes" column in its annually published *Statistics*

A 1950s view of the Murphy Building, which was used as the city hall and by Falls Church Public Library. *FCPL Photographic Archive.*

of Virginia Public Libraries. In the 1944–45 report, County Librarian Margaret Edwards reported that FCPL did not provide service to Black residents. A note in the report specifies that her answer included the town libraries of Falls Church, Fairfax, Herndon and McLean. Even if Black residents could have accessed the library, an additional limit that Falls Church Library enforced on its citizens was that every library card applicant was required to have the signature of another Falls Church resident on the card.[183]

In November 1948, the Falls Church Library left the old Congregational Church building and moved into two rooms in the Murphy Building at 151 East Broad Street. The following April, the now-incorporated City of Falls Church created a library board of trustees composed of five members to oversee its library's management and policies. Now officially a city institution, the library received regular appropriations and no longer required the sponsorship of the women's club.[184] In October 1949, the library board appointed Jewel Drickamer as its first full-time certified librarian.[185] It was around this time that the library's access to Black residents seems to have started.

Falls Church's War on Comic Books

In 1949, Mrs. Flora M. Coan led a citywide effort to prevent children from reading violent comic books in Falls Church. Having read a report released by the American Bar Association about a correlation between comic books and juvenile delinquency, the mother of eight was stirred to action. She roused women in her church and received assistance from the parent-teacher association in convincing Falls Church merchants to remove the most sinister comic books from their shelves. Eventually, the initiative reached the city council, and Mayor Albert M. Orme appointed a Committee on More and Better Reading.

The committee established an aggressive reading campaign, with the philosophy that if the city's children spent more time reading better books, they would have less time to read comics. The Falls Church Public Library was incorporated into the campaign, and Jewel Drickamer, the librarian, worked closely with the committee. Fifteen women from the PTA volunteered in the library, engaging with children about the stories they read and providing them with book recommendations. The library also initiated a daily story hour and featured lists of books recommended by students who had formed a junior board of review.

Left: Albert M. Orme served two terms as Falls Church mayor and pushed a city expansion program from 1948 to 1951. He established the Committee on More and Better Reading to encourage Falls Church children to read quality literature instead of violent comic books. *FCPL Photographic Archive.*

Below: Students in James Lee Elementary School's cafeteria in May 1953. *Fairfax County Public Schools.*

In the summer of 1949, the mayor's committee started a seasonal reading program that ended with Mayor Orme personally presenting certificates to each child who read ten or more books from a selected list. Each school in Falls Church participated and planned its own reading program.

The James Lee Elementary School, built by Fairfax County Public Schools in 1948 to replace the aged and inadequate Falls Church Colored School, joined the mayor's second reading program in the winter of 1949. That season's program concluded with a ceremony at James Lee School on May 19, 1950, during which Mayor Orme awarded certificates.[186] Later that year, Willis Milner Richards of the James Lee School was one of three children who won the committee's citywide poster contest for submitting the best drawing of "Falls Church Freddie," a cartoon character who typified better reading. It is not clear whether Black children could access the public library during this initiative.

The General Federation of Women's Clubs chose Falls Church's reading program as one of three outstanding "better entertainment for children projects" in the nation. "School libraries, public and parochial, elementary and high, white and colored, join in the 'better reading' program," reported the *Fairfax Standard* in May 1950.[187] The mayor's Committee for More and Better Reading was a biracial organization. Chaired by Flora Coan, who had been the instigator for the movement, the committee had ten members appointed by Mayor Orme, including Reverend Wallace Earl Costner.

Reverend Wallace E. Costner

As pastor of the Second Baptist Church, Reverend Wallace E. Costner (1895–1971) was one of the most respected voices in Falls Church's Black community. He would go out of his way to help anyone, whether he knew them or not. Costner also used the pulpit to fight for civil rights, particularly equality in public schools.

"Reverend Costner was a great leader and was well known in the courts in Fairfax County and highly respected. He was just a very, very nice pastor," recalled Falls Church resident Juanita Smith in 2005. According to her recollections, Costner and another Falls Church civil rights activist, Ollie Tinner, "went to a lot of the meetings from the county, and they would let everybody know what the rulings were, what the laws were and the changes and so forth. And they helped with a lot of legal things that had to be done in the community."[188]

Costner, born in 1895, initially hailed from Kings Mountain, North Carolina. After serving in World War I, he settled in Washington, D.C., where he worked in the U.S. Government Printing Office. In 1929, he was a member of the first class to graduate from the Washington Baptist Seminary. His first assignment after ordination was at Purcellville's Mt. Zoar Baptist Church, followed by a dual appointment at Warner Baptist Church in Bailey's Crossroads. He left both posts to take on the pastorate of the Second Baptist Church in Falls Church in April 1935, and he remained the pastor there until his death in 1971.[189]

Reverend Wallace E. Costner, a longtime pastor of Second Baptist Church in Falls Church, tirelessly fought for equal education for Black children in Fairfax County. *FCPL Photographic Archive.*

Shortly after taking on his new assignment, in 1936, Costner purchased a house for his family on Virginia Avenue, across from what would become the future permanent home of Falls Church Public Library. He quickly became a noted local civic leader and was elected president of the Fairfax County Colored Citizens' Association, which had five hundred members at the time. He advocated for the equal education of Black children in Fairfax County and often appeared before the school board, requesting better facilities for Black students and teachers. His pleas were almost always ignored or tabled.

In February 1942, Costner appeared before the school board with the Falls Church Colored School League, imploring the board to construct a modern three-room school for the Black children of Falls Church on a vacant parcel of land that had been purchased years earlier. Costner emphasized the poor conditions of the existing Falls Church Colored School, including dim lighting and unusable toilets. Unwilling to include the cost of building a new school in the upcoming budget, the board directed that the school be repaired instead.

Costner and the Falls Church Colored School League returned to the school board in 1944, urging the same request, but they were again rebuffed. It was not until August 1946 that the school board authorized that a new school be built on property, which had formerly been owned by James Lee, a Black man who was born free in 1839. Lee's son sold a portion of the property for the construction of the school, and it was named in his father's honor. On February 6, 1948, James Lee Elementary School opened its

Top: Built in 1892, the Falls Church Colored School served the Black community until 1948. *FCPL Photographic Archive.*

Bottom: In 1948, James Lee Elementary School replaced the aging inadequate Falls Church Colored School. It was the first Black school in Fairfax County to have individual classrooms for each of its grades. *FCPL Photographic Archive.*

doors. It was the first modern school for Black children in Fairfax County, with a library, cafeteria, clinic, auditorium, indoor plumbing and individual classrooms for each grade.[190]

For nearly a decade, Costner also fought for the construction of an all-Black high school in Fairfax County. Black students, at a cost to their parents, had to either travel to Washington, D.C., or Manassas to attend high school. Some students were travelling as far as ninety miles roundtrip each day to get to the Regional High School in Manassas.

At a school board meeting on March 9, 1948, Costner acted as chairman for a group of eleven Black citizens who held meetings to discuss the need for a Black high school in Fairfax County. Reverend Costner read a resolution that was adopted at those meetings to the board, requesting a modern high school be built for the county's Black children. "A first-class comprehensive high school will lift the level of intelligence for all colored citizens," read Costner. "It will keep more children in school and will attract colored residents to the county who will be a great asset."[191] Another five years would pass before Luther Jackson High School opened in Merrifield as the county's first Black high school in 1954.

Luther Jackson High School in Merrifield, Virginia, on August 18, 1954. *FCPL Photographic Archive.*

Throughout the 1940s and 1950s, Costner maintained numerous leadership positions and helped organize the King Tyre Lodge, a Black Masonic chapter, in Falls Church in 1946. The following year, he became the first Black man elected to a Democratic Central Committee south of the Mason-Dixon line.[192] Throughout his tireless civic work for the community, he joined forces with Falls Church's most well-known civil rights leader, Dr. Edwin B. Henderson, a member of Costner's Second Baptist Church. Together, they worked to desegregate the schools and Falls Church Public Library.

DR. EDWIN B. HENDERSON

Edwin B. Henderson, the "father of Black basketball," cofounded the Fairfax County branch of the NAACP and served twice as the president of the Virginia NAACP. *FCPL Photographic Archive.*

Dr. Edwin Bancroft Henderson (1883–1977) spent a lifetime championing equal rights in the Washington metropolitan region. Born in 1883 in Washington, D.C., Henderson graduated from Dunbar High School and was first in his class at Miner Teachers College.[193] In the fall of 1904, he became the first certified Black male instructor of physical education employed in the United States after accepting a job with the D.C. school system. After a fifty-year career there, he retired in 1954 as the director of health and physical education for Washington's Black schools.

Beginning in the summer of 1904, Henderson studied physical education at Harvard University's Summer School Physical Training. It was there that he learned the new game of basketball from the people that James Naismith, the inventor of the game, first taught in the 1890s. Henderson brought the game back to Washington, D.C., and introduced it to Black students.

In 1907, Henderson and his future brother-in-law dropped into the white-only Central YMCA to watch a basketball game, but the two were asked to leave after sitting down. The experience inspired Henderson to start a league of his own, and in December that year, the first known Black-only basketball game occurred at True Reformer's Hall on U Street. Henderson saw sports as a means for Black people to debunk the notion of racial inferiority and open doors of opportunity. He subsequently organized the Twelfth Street YMCA basketball team and won the 1909–10 Colored Basketball Championship.

Henderson played his last organized basketball game on Christmas Day 1910. The previous day, he had married Mary Ellen "Nellie" Meriweather, who asked him to stop playing over concerns for his wellbeing.[194] The couple moved to Falls Church, where his grandmother Eliza Henderson, formerly enslaved, had lived since emancipation. Henderson visited her often as a child. While growing up, he had witnessed a changing racial landscape in the nation's capital. Originally able to patronize theaters, ride unsegregated streetcars and walk into restaurants to order a sandwich, Henderson viewed firsthand the ugly rise of Jim Crow in the District during the Wilson administration. He later recalled in 1965:

> *I felt terrible, and I must admit that I could almost have been a disloyal American the way it affected me, particularly after I moved to Virginia, when my son and all of us had to ride on the Jim Crow cars, and he began to question me why he couldn't sit here, and I said I was boiling mad and very frustrated.*[195]

On November 9, 1914, Mary Riley Styles's husband, Samuel Styles, a councilman on the Falls Church Town Council, co-introduced a segregation ordinance, along with Dr. Reginal Munson, that made it unlawful for Black residents to buy, sell or rent property within a certain area in town. The proposed ordinance did not receive enough votes and failed; however, at the next town council meeting on December 14, 1914, they learned that the Virginia General Assembly had earlier passed an optional law in March 1912 that allowed towns to segregate residential districts. A segregation ordinance was proposed again and unanimously passed, making Falls Church the only town in Northern Virginia to make use of the state's law.

Outraged, Henderson called together some of the town's leading Black citizens, who met in the home of Joseph B. Tinner on January 8, 1915. They formed the Colored Citizens Protective League (CCPL) to protest the passage of the ordinance. Three days later, Henderson and three others attended the town council's meeting to personally convey their objections. The council agreed to take their opinion into consideration, dismissed the group and, upon reconsidering the vote, passed the ordinance again.[196]

The CCPL met again on January 18 and agreed to write a letter imploring the town council to repeal the ordinance and request information from the NAACP about organizing a branch in the town. The league also wrote letters to Falls Church citizens imploring them not to approve the segregation ordinance that was on an upcoming ballot on May 25, 1915. "Must we, as citizens, suffer a change by permitting men whose views are warped by the traditions and prejudices of human slavery to dictate new policy?" wrote Henderson. The majority of the town's voters approved the ordinance, and a boundary map was accepted for segregating the town's 113 Black residents and 1,212 white residents.[197]

The CCPL sued the town to prevent the enforcement of the ordinance and ultimately prevailed. Consequently, the NAACP approved the formation of a Falls Church branch. The CCPL merged into the NACCP Falls Church and Vicinity branch, becoming the first rural branch of the organization in June 1918, with Henderson elected as its secretary. The group morphed into the Fairfax County chapter of the NAACP when it was chartered in 1944. Both Henderson and Costner were involved in the organization, which had many successes in combating Jim Crow. Henderson later recalled in 1965:

> While I was teaching school, people thought that I had a lot of nerve, but it was just natural to me to be always protesting against anything I thought was inhuman and against the dignity of people.[198]

FALLS CHURCH LIBRARY DESEGREGATES

Pinpointing when Black residents were officially allowed to access the library is difficult. The earliest mention that Falls Church Public Library was desegregated appears in library board minutes from a meeting held on June 11, 1953, when the group discussed prospects for building a permanent library. John Bold, a former board member, attended the meeting and presented fundraising ideas for the initiative. The minutes reported:

> He suggests that we make up a brochure, which would include the historical interest of the community, the ratio of reading, the Great Books programs, the per capita expenditure for the library, the educational background in Falls Church and the fact that the library operates on a non-segregated basis.[199]

Three years prior to that meeting, on March 13, 1950, the Falls Church Public Library held its first "Local Authors Night," which indicates it may have been desegregated then. Librarian Jewel Drickamer sent invitations to twenty-two local authors, including E.B. Henderson, to speak with visitors. "Edwin Bancroft Henderson, whose *The Negro in Sports* was published recently, has also been asked to attend and give a short talk on his book," reported the *Fairfax Standard*.[200] The invited authors had their books and magazine articles on display in the library for the entire week, and Mayor Albert Orme was on hand to welcome guests to the open house. Eleven authors showed up for the event, but it is unknown whether Henderson accepted the invitation and made an appearance. His book, however, was featured in the weeklong display.

Around that same time, Arthur B. McLean, a chairman of the Falls Church Public Library Board of Trustees, requested that the Extension Division of the state library conduct an appraisal of the library's condition and services. Christine Coffey, an assistant Extension librarian, presented her findings to the board in May 1950. She determined the library suffered from a lack of space and qualified staff, poor financing and a weak book collection. Coffey offered remedies to these concerns in her report and urged the board to "cooperate with libraries in adjoining areas to the end that library service is available to all the people wherever they live."[201]

Due to an expiring lease in the Murphy Building, the library was forced to relocate once again in September 1950. It moved into the Ellison House, an old antebellum mansion at 934 West Broad Street, but this space, too, quickly became cramped and inadequate.[202] A 1951 promotional pamphlet for the library explicitly stated, "Anyone six and over may have a card," although it is unclear if the library was truly inclusive to everyone.

In the summer of 1950, Kay Martin Britto, a high school student, started working as a page in the Falls Church Library. She grew up in Falls Church and attended Saint James Catholic School. Her ninth-grade glass at Immaculata High School in Washington, D.C., was the school's first class to be integrated in 1950. While working in the library, she mainly shelved books, but staff eventually allowed her to work at the library's circulation desk. Britto worked one evening per week, every Saturday, and during her summer vacations until she was a freshman at Mary Washington College in 1955.

"I have no real recollections of an African American entering the library," Britto recalled in April 2022. "In my memory, there was no serving of any African American patrons in the library while I was there. It was the norms of the day."[203] She recalled Falls Church as being an extremely segregated town. While Britto was employed by the library, her father, James Oliver Martin, was appointed to a three-year term on the library board in 1952. After graduating college, Britto went on to work as a professional librarian for Arlington and Fairfax County Public Libraries.

A presentation of books occurred in the Lions' Den of the Falls Church Public Library, then located in the old Ellison House, on January 10, 1953. *Mary Riley Styles Public Library, Local History Collection, Falls Church, VA.*

Even if Black citizens were able to use the library at this time, further limitations were enacted in July 1954. The library board voted to charge all out-of-city residents a five-dollar annual fee; 62 percent of the library's borrowers resided in Fairfax County, and the FCPL Library Board rejected carrying some of the load for Falls Church by offering financial assistance.[204] Since most Black residents lived outside the city limits, this would have hindered their library access.

In January 1955, the library and its fifteen thousand books were displaced once again and moved into a brand-new rented two-story red brick house at 201 East Broad Street. Simultaneously, the library acquired a new librarian, Elizabeth M. Shaw. On August 19, 1955, Shaw prepared a report for a regional fiscal survey, which indicated inclusion: "The services of the Library are free to all citizens of Falls Church and to persons employed by the city or employed in the city."[205] She also wrote that one of the library's goals for 1955–60 was to increase its public relations program "to make all citizens realize [the] vital role of [the] library in their lives and that it belongs to them."[206]

The following month was the first time that the Falls Church Public Library Board of Trustees went on record, explicitly offering service to Black residents. The minutes of the board meeting on September 28, 1955, recorded:

> *Board members would like to have Mrs.* [Elizabeth] *Graham pursue the matter of the library's service to the colored people of Falls Church by contacting Mr. Costner and Mr. Henderson.*[207]

The issue seems to have arisen in response to an earlier inquiry from Costner and Henderson. Elizabeth Graham had been on the library's staff since 1951. She reported on her meeting with the two civil rights leaders at the library board meeting on November 10, 1955. The three had discussed the best ways to serve the community's Black children and adults. Henderson brought some historical materials to the meeting, which he gave to Graham to be added to the library's Virginiana collection on local history, which had been established in 1952. The meeting minutes continued:

> *Mrs.* [June] *Bonnell moved that Mrs.* [Martha] *Delaney contact the principals of the schools attended by Falls Church Negro children to offer these children the same services now being given other city school children, e.g. group visits to the library. At this time, the library services can be explained to them, and they may have an opportunity to make application for a reader's card. The motion was approved unanimously.*[208]

At the next board meeting on December 7, 1955, librarian Elizabeth M. Shaw provided a report of the library's efforts to arrange school visits for Falls Church's Black children attending Fairfax County Public Schools. A motion was passed to obtain a list of addresses of the children and the names of their parents so that a letter could be sent to remind them that they were entitled to use the library's services. After some discussion, the motion was tabled for a month.[209] The proposed initiative never appears in the minutes again.

The next day, December 8, 1955, Henderson spoke before two hundred parents and teachers at the Parker-Gray High School in Alexandria during the closing session of the twenty-eighth annual Conference of the Virginia Congress of Colored Parents and Teachers. Henderson called for the prompt integration of schools in the South. The *Washington Post* covered his remarks: "He urged teachers and parents to 'force open public libraries' to Negro children as a means of shortening the educational gap between white and colored children. 'This is part of our new responsibility,' he added."[210]

The same day, Jean Strup, the corresponding secretary for the Falls Church Public Library Board of Trustees, mailed a letter of thanks to Henderson:

> The board of trustees of the library has asked me to thank you for your contribution of materials for the Virginia collection. We have found it very interesting, and it will add to our growing collection of Falls Church archives.[211]

Following the interaction with Henderson and Costner, the library board began incorporating inclusive language in its policy documents. In September 1956, a book selection policy for the library read, "The Falls Church Public Library provides, on equal terms, free service to all individuals and groups in the community, both children and adults."[212] This was reemphasized in the library's 1957 policy and procedure manual accepted by the library board: "The Falls Church Public Library provides free library service to all individuals and groups in the community."[213]

Despite desegregation, local Black educators still faced obstacles when obtaining access to the library. Costner reached out to the library board, inquiring about borrowing privileges for teachers at the James Lee School who seemingly were unable to check out books. The librarian Elizabeth Shaw wrote to him on March 16, 1958:

> Dear Mr. Costner:
>
> I am very happy to be able to report to you that the board of trustees of the Falls Church Public Library made the following resolution at its meeting last night:
>
> Resolved: That a teacher in the Fairfax County Public School system who is actually teaching children who reside within the corporate limits of the city of Falls Church and who would not otherwise be entitled to a free borrower's card at the Falls Church Public Library because of non-residence within the corporate limits of the city is hereby entitled to a free borrower's card in the Falls Church Public Library upon application and the presentation of proper identification.
>
> It is my thought that you may wish to personally convey this information to the proper persons at the James Lee and Luther Jackson Schools.[214]

BUILDING A PERMANENT HOME
FOR THE FALLS CHURCH LIBRARY

Meanwhile, the Library Board had been meeting with architect J. Russell Bailey to plan a new permanent library building. In April 1953, Francis and Elizabeth Styles, the children of longtime library committee chairman Mary Riley Styles, gifted a 150-square-foot lot at the corner of Park and Virginia Avenues to be used as the library's site. After her mother's death, Elizabeth Styles carried on the family's tradition of supporting the library, having been appointed to the library board in October 1952.[215] Like her mother, she had been dedicated to improving the city and was engaged with local civic affairs and clubs, including the United Daughters of the Confederacy. The Riley estate's parcel was gifted as a living memorial in honor of Styles's mother. Falls Church officials, the library board and the Styles family held a groundbreaking ceremony for the $210,000 permanent library building on August 18, 1957.[216]

However, the construction of the library could only be financed by a bond issue. Consequently, the Friends of the Library, which had formed in 1951, organized a citywide campaign to raise support for construction. On October 10, 1956, the library board held a citywide public meeting in the Madison School auditorium to encourage residents to vote "yes" on the upcoming library bond. John D.T. Bold, a chairman of the library board, gave a speech to rally the voters:

> *First, it is basic with us that the library is your library. It belongs to you, and the only justification for the existence of the board of trustees and the library is to serve you, and all of you, from the toddlers to the oldsters, regardless of class, or creed, or color, and regardless of your educational or cultural background or lack of such background.*

The bond successfully passed on November 6, 1957, and construction began immediately. The city dedicated the brand-new two-story library containing twenty-three thousand books and a modern city hall building a half-block away in a three-day celebration, beginning with a ceremony on July 4, 1958. Over five hundred people attended, including congressmen, politicians, city officials, businessmen and Virginia's state librarian Randolph W. Church, who gave the keynote speech.[217]

Also attending the ceremony was E.B. Henderson and his wife, Mary E. Henderson. He had been involved with planning the dedication ceremonies through assisting the publicity committee.[218] The couple both

The groundbreaking for the new permanent Falls Church Public Library. *From left to right*: Mayor Herman Fink, library chairman June Bonnell, Elizabeth Styles and Francis Styles. *D.C. Public Library, Star Collection* © Washington Post.

signed the guestbook on opening day in a historical exhibit featured in the library's basement. Shortly thereafter, E.B. Henderson reflected on the library's dedication:

> *No intelligent negro accepts segregation as the American way of life. Having worked hard in his community and having offered his life in wars for the defense of democracy and his nation, he intends to press onward towards full realization of the goal of complete citizenship. Until the barrier of color or races is removed, which limits his opportunity for employment, access to public accommodations and deserving first-class citizenship, the sensitive negro will continue to strive for his constitutional rights. The dedication of our new city hall and library have meanings as civilizing justice and law and education to supplant ignorance and prejudice. Negro citizens, therefore, are equally proud of our new library and city hall, which they, too, helped erect.*[219]

The Falls Church Library's success received international coverage upon opening. In 1959, the United States Information Service featured the library as the perfect example of a small U.S. library in a *USIS Feature* press release that was distributed to newspapers, magazines and radio stations. The article chronicled the library's origins and described its various users. "Through its arched doorway, in the course of a day, stream many kinds of people, young and old, Negro and white."[220] Accompanying the release were four photographs, including one of a Black man sitting at a table using a library book. The image was published in a Venezuelan newspaper called *La Esfera*.[221]

RACIAL BARRIERS COLLAPSE IN FALLS CHURCH

Despite "Massive Resistance" against integrating public schools in Virginia following the 1954 Supreme Court case *Brown v. Board of Education*, Falls Church became the first Virginia city to voluntarily integrate its school system in 1961. Reverend Wallace Costner, whose daughter Marion Costner was one of the first Black students integrated into the George Mason Junior-Senior High School, was invited to give the invocation during the dedication ceremonies for the school's new addition on October 5, 1963.[222]

Costner appeared alongside former Virginia Governor James Lindsay Almond Jr., who gave his first formal address since leaving office. The two men could not have been more opposite. Almond had supported "Massive Resistance" as Virginia's governor from 1958 to 1962, while Costner had fiercely combated that policy. That same year, Costner and his daughter Marion participated in protests that resulted in the full desegregation of Falls Church's State Theatre.[223]

In 1963, the American Library Association published a survey report titled "Access to Public Libraries." The study sought to examine the scope and extent to which racial segregation affected access to public libraries throughout the South. Richard Burns, who had been the Falls Church librarian since 1960, wrote a review of the report in the December 15, 1963 *Library Journal*, challenging his colleagues to question their professional ethics and eradicate unequitable policies.

"This report has exposed a ghost in our purpose," wrote Burns. "This ghost is known by many aliases: apathy, cowardice, conformity, weakness, lack of political imagination, expediency, ignorance, inability, security and defeatism. By any name, this ghost is a poison infecting the spirit of our profession. The critical question prompted by this report never appears in its text: *Shall we go on poisoning ourselves?*"[224]

The following year, the Falls Church Public Library became the first public library in Virginia to publish a book and the smallest library in the country to turn publisher in 1964.[225] After years of extensive research by historian Melvin Lee Steadman Jr., the library published his book *Falls Church: By Fence and Fireside*. The 640-page historical and genealogical account of Falls Church was the first major history written about the city, but it primarily covered white businesses, citizens and families. Black contributions to the city's history were condensed into a single chapter at the end of the historical narrative.

The Falls Church Public Library, however, did try to better preserve local Black history. On April 25, 1965, it held a kick-off event called "An Hour of History, Vol. 1. No. 1" to celebrate National Library Week. That evening, a panel of five participants gathered in the library to discuss and record an oral history of Falls Church for posterity. Library board member Mel Bolster moderated the biracial panel, which included E.B. Henderson, former councilman Charles Gage, City Manager Harry E. Wells, George Mason High School student Michael Cone and Falls Church historian Melvin L. Steadman Jr.[226]

An oral history panel at the library in April 1965. *From left to right*: Charles E. Gage, Edwin B. Henderson, Mel Bolster, Michael Cone, Harry Wells and Reverend Melvin L. Steadman. *Mary Riley Styles Public Library, Local History Collection, Falls Church, VA.*

Eighty citizens gathered to hear Henderson reminisce about life in Falls Church during the 1890s. He also spoke of the handsome holly tree in front of the library. The city had purchased it from Henderson, who had acquired it from the former property of Frederick Foote in Seven Corners. The Foote family were some of the earliest Black settlers in Falls Church, and every Christmas, Frederick Foote tied a string and bell to the tree to discourage anyone from stealing it.[227]

In December 1965, an unidentified reporter from the *Falls Church Globe* wandered into the Falls Church Public Library and interviewed several patrons using the facility. While there, he encountered Janice Ashley, a recent graduate from the segregated Luther Jackson High School, which had closed six months earlier due to the integration of Fairfax County Public Schools. During the high school's final year, Ashley served on the library committee as a senior. She assisted the school's librarian Mabel Mosley with repairing books, collecting overdue fines from students, reshelving materials and charging and discharging library books. Now a freshman at Howard University, Ashley frequently used Falls Church Public Library, finding it an easy place to study. "The TV and record player don't bother you in here," she explained.[228] At the time, she lived less than a mile from the library, and it became a convenient escape when her noisy high school–age brother came home.

The Falls Church Public Library, now known as the Mary Riley Styles Public Library, has come a long way since librarian Elizabeth Graham met with Costner and Henderson to provide more equitable service to the city's Black citizens. In June 2020, in response to the murder of George Floyd in Minneapolis, Jennifer Carroll, the library director for Mary Riley

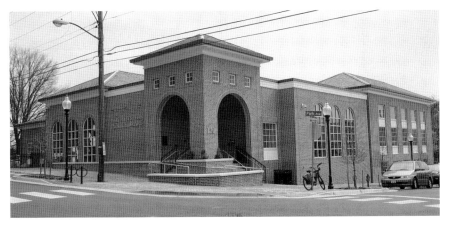

The Mary Riley Styles Public Library as it appeared in 2022. *Authors' photograph.*

Styles Public Library, issued a written statement to the city's residents: "How we treat the African American community is all of our responsibility and concern....Libraries are not excluded from discriminatory treatment of African Americans, both from a historical perspective and the current struggle to diversify library staff and literature."[229] Carroll reemphasized the library's commitment to promoting justice and peace.

The library board of trustees issued a statement of its own, fully commending and supporting Carroll:

> We enthusiastically support her efforts to use our library to help address those issues forthrightly, through open dialogue and through increasing resources and books that may help guide us forward. Our communities' libraries share the guiding principles of accessibility, equity, inclusivity, education, intellectual freedom and a welcoming environment for all. We are committed to upholding these tenets and actively standing against discrimination and racism.[230]

Throughout 2020 and 2021, Mary Riley Styles Public Library sponsored a community conversation series that featured panels with local experts on police reform, racial bullying, affordable housing and the history of segregated schools. The library board also extensively reviewed its library procedures and policies to make the library a more diverse, inclusive and equitable space.[231]

During that process, the board voted to eliminate overdue fines and printing fees as financial barriers to library access. "Ending overdue fines supports our mission; the library is open and accessible to all members of our community," said Carroll.[232] The year ended with a ribbon-cutting of the renovated and greatly expanded library building on September 10, 2021. What had started 122 years earlier as a segregated library in a small outbuilding in George Hawxhurst's backyard is now a state-of-the-art public library that welcomes everyone.

RECOGNITION

In 1963, the road that leads to the Second Baptist Church, where Reverend Wallace Costner was pastor for thirty-six years, was renamed Costner Drive. A renewed effort to recognize the "grandfather of Black basketball" has gained momentum, led by his grandson Edwin B. Henderson II and his wife, Nikki. In 2013, Henderson was finally acknowledged for introducing the game of basketball to Black youth and was inducted into the Naismith Memorial Basketball Hall of Fame. His alma mater, the University of the District of Columbia, renamed its athletic facility the Dr. Edwin Bancroft Henderson Sports Complex in February 2022 and launched the Dr. Edwin Bancroft Henderson Memorial Fund to honor his legacy with scholarships and a planned permanent memorial on the campus. That same month, the Washington Wizards, who play about two miles south from the True Reformer building on U Street, where Henderson staged the first-ever all-Black basketball game, named its philanthropic team player award after him.

Locally, the Providence Recreation Center in Falls Church was dedicated in Henderson's honor in 1982. In 1999, the Tinner Hill Heritage Foundation, whose mission is to preserve and promote the history of civil rights leaders in Falls Church and the surrounding areas, erected two memorials in Tinner Hill Park honoring its Black leaders, including Henderson. On November 20, 2021, a state historical marker was unveiled in front of Henderson's former residence. The Mary Ellen Henderson Middle School, named for Henderson's wife, a longtime teacher at the Falls Church Colored School and civil rights pioneer herself, opened in 2005.

Existing Sites

The Site of Falls Church Public Library (1913–unknown, 1919–1948)
222 North Washington Street, Falls Church, VA 22046

The old Congregational Church building, built in 1879, was the third home of the Falls Church Public Library, beginning in 1913. The library eventually moved out but returned in 1919 and remained there for almost thirty years. Black residents were unable to access the library during its entire tenure here. The building is now home to the Center for Spiritual Enlightenment.

The Site of Falls Church Public Library (1955–1958)
201 East Broad Street, Falls Church, VA 22046

The Falls Church Public Library moved into this newly constructed house in January 1955. It would become the library's final temporary quarters before it moved into a permanent library building in 1958. Although the

Falls Church Public Library called the old Congregational Church building home for many years. Today, it is the Center for Spiritual Enlightenment. *Authors' photograph.*

Falls Church Public Library temporarily relocated into this brand-new house in 1955 before moving into its permanent home in 1958. Today, this house is a private residence. *Authors' photograph.*

library was recorded as being desegregated in 1953, it was at this location when E.B. Henderson and Reverend Wallace Costner met with librarian Elizabeth Graham to discuss developing better access for Black residents in 1955. Today, the house is a private residence.

Mary Riley Styles Public Library
120 North Virginia Avenue, Falls Church, VA 22046

Renamed the Mary Riley Styles Public Library in 1977, the first permanent home of Falls Church Public Library was dedicated on July 4, 1958. After several renovations and expansions in 1969, 1992 and 2021, it continues to be the city's only public library.

LOUDOUN COUNTY

*T*oday's Loudoun County Public Library, founded in 1973, was preceded by Purcellville Library, founded in 1938, the only public library in Loudoun at the time. From its inception, the library was for white residents only. Purcellville Library's board had ignored the 1946 state mandate to provide service to all residents, as well as multiple requests from both Black and white citizens to provide bookmobile services to Black residents. Integration only occurred after legal action was initiated by a Black couple who also happened to be working as decorators for President Dwight Eisenhower's sister-in-law. Thanks to their activism, the Purcellville Library would become the first public building to be desegregated in Loudoun County.

THE MURRAYS

Samuel Cardoza Murray (1915–1998) and Josie Cook Murray (1920–2010) were respected and well-liked citizens of Purcellville.[233] Their talent for sewing and building everything from dolls to furniture had culminated in them opening their own upholstery shop. "They owned a van they used to pick up and deliver the furniture pieces that they repaired and recovered. Josie did excellent seamstress/reupholstery work. They were very soft spoken, gentle people," recalled former Purcellville resident A.J. Roberts.

Samuel and Josie Murray with their son, Samuel Keith Murray, 1950. When prevented from checking out a book at Purcellville Library, the Murrays took legal action, resulting in the desegregation of the library. *Winslow Williams Photograph Collection (VC 0003) Rust Archive, Thomas Balch Library, Leesburg, VA.*

Both the Cook and Murray families had lived in Loudoun for generations, producing several prominent members of the Black community. Known for the quality of their work, the Murrays had created home décor for both Black and white residents, including prominent citizens, such as Senator Everett Dirkson.[234]

In 1956, First Lady Mamie Eisenhower's sister, Mabel Frances "Mike" Moore, who lived near Hillsboro, commissioned the Murrays to create window treatments for her home. The couple went to the library to research the Austrian-style window shades Moore requested. They were informed that they could not check out books due to their race.

Librarian Barbara Graham referred them to the chairman of the Purcellville Library Board Oscar L. Emerick, who said that it "would not be in the spirit of the citizens who organized the library" for the Murrays to check out a book. At this time, a Black resident who wanted to check out a book would need to have a white resident check it out for them. Emerick offered to check out the book for the Murrays but said he could not let them check the book out themselves.[235]

Mr. Murray, who was forty-two years old at the time, objected to not being allowed to check out the book in his own name. "If I didn't pay my taxes, they would sell my home. Since I do pay my taxes, I felt I should have the use of the book from the library, which is paid for by my taxes," Mr. Murray told a reporter.[236] Mrs. Murray supported the decision. The Murrays found a lawyer, Oliver Ellis Stone of Alexandria, who agreed to take their case after several other attorneys turned it down.

The Community Study Group, an integrated civic group that included members from Goose Creek Friends in nearby Lincoln, offered to help fund the lawsuit, but Mr. Murray said he and his wife would pay for everything themselves.[237] Stone had advised them that accepting outside donations would be detrimental to the case.[238]

In February 1957, Stone wrote to the library board, pointing out that Virginia law specified libraries must serve all residents if they were to be supported by state taxes. After consulting authorities at the town and county levels and confirming that funding from those sources was also at stake, the library board voted 7–5 in favor of integration on March 21, 1957. The decision states the library would be open to all "irrespective of race or color" and that the bookmobile service would be extended to Black residents by September 1957.[239]

But segregationists—calling themselves "Defenders of State Sovereignty and Individual Liberty"—refused to concede. Meetings and impassioned speeches followed, during which segregationists vowed to either close the library or move it to private ownership to avoid integration.

The "Loudoun Defenders," as the segregationists were nicknamed, circulated a petition to support their cause and received 44 signatures, compared to 366 signatures on a counterpetition.[240] This seems to indicate their views did not represent the majority opinion at the time. Tom Burke, a *Washington Star* reporter, indicated that Purcellville was out of step with the rest of the region, writing: "Library facilities are open to colored residents in Fairfax and Arlington Counties and the cities of Alexandria and Falls Church."[241]

The drama surrounding the Loudoun County Board of Supervisors' vote to fund the library, which would entail integration, included the tie-breaking voter calling in sick. Commonwealth attorney Sterling M. Harrison was then called on to break the tie. Harrison, who was the president of the Loudoun Defenders, also excused himself from voting and had his secretary report

The living room of the Eisenhower home in Gettysburg, Pennsylvania, features the Austrian-style window sheers that the Murrays were researching when they encountered discrimination in the Purcellville Library. *National Park Service, Eisenhower National Historic Site.*

that he was ill. The supervisors then voted again, and S.D. Phillips, who had been on the fence, changed his vote, resulting in a 4–2 decision in favor of the library appropriation, thus assuring integration.

After the ordeal and surrounding publicity, the library board voted to ban reporters from attending board meetings and from accessing the board minutes. By a vote of 5–3, it also rejected an alternative that would have allowed representatives from two county newspapers to view minutes on request.[242]

During the controversy, white customers continued to treat the Murrays respectfully at their shop, but others, including the Purcellville town deputy, tried to intimidate them. One day, the deputy himself led a line of fifteen cars, which drove slowly with horns blaring, past the Murrays' home. When the Murrays complained, "the deputy said the group was just teenagers who wanted to show the Murrays how well they could drive."[243]

Poignantly, after the 1957 desegregation of Purcellville Library, it remained largely unused by Black residents.[244] According to an article published in the *Loudoun Times-Mirror* newspaper a week after the desegregation vote: "Since Thursday's vote, one Negro woman and her young daughter have registered as members and have taken out books."[245] The fact that only one woman with a child ventured to use the library after such a well-publicized case (covered by both Black and white newspapers at the time) indicates that most Black residents did not feel comfortable or welcome to use the library, even after the formal desegregation. Nevertheless, it was a historic victory for the civil rights movement in Loudoun County.

The Murrays were now free to engage in research and complete their decorating job for Mrs. Moore. President and First Lady Eisenhower were so impressed when they saw the shades hanging at the Moores' home, they requested the Murrays create similar window treatments, as well as chairs and other furnishings, for their farm near Gettysburg.[246] That property, now known as Eisenhower National Historic Site, is operated by the National Park Service and open to the public.[247] Austrian-style window shades can be seen in many rooms of the home.

Purcellville Library's Bookmobile

Purcellville Library's bookmobile served only white residents prior to the Murrays' legal action. Bookmobile outreach to Black residents had been discussed previously by the library board and town council, but no action had been taken.[248] The library board had tabled numerous requests, including a 1953 request from Alfred K. Talbot, the principal of the Carver School, to provide bookmobile service to his students; a 1955 letter from the

Purcellville Library's bookmobile, 1946. *Winslow Williams Photograph Collection (VC 0003) Rust Archive, Thomas Balch Library, Leesburg, VA.*

Quaker Society of Friends; and a 1956 appeal from Richard W. Johnson, the secretary of the Loudoun County Ministerial Association.[249] The requests to serve Black communities had come from both Black and white residents, including some board of trustees members—but to no avail.

However, librarian Jean Caulkins Carruthers (1919–1985), who worked for Purcellville Library for thirty-eight years, took it upon herself to quietly deliver books to Black residents during the 1950s, despite the segregation policy, according to Ed Nichols, a town council member.[250] After the Murrays' actions resulted in the desegregation of the library building, the bookmobile also began officially serving Black and white customers.

Thomas Balch Library and Black Library Staff During Segregation

The Thomas Balch Library in Leesburg operated for fifty years as a subscription library, opening in its present location in 1922 and becoming a public-but-segregated library in 1960. The library is named for Thomas Balch (1821–1877), a Leesburg native, and its operation was supported by an endowment established by his sons. According to the library's website, the library was desegregated in 1965; however, current staff report that the exact date is uncertain.

Gene Ashton (born in 1946), a Black high school student, was recruited to work at Thomas Balch Library and remained employed there from 1963 to 1964.[251] Ashton reported that he was supplied with a library card and was treated with warmth and respect by the staff. He was entrusted with the keys to the library. However, he reported that he did not see any other Black adults or children using the library for the duration of his employment there—a fact he attributes to the discomfort felt by those who were previously excluded from the facility.[252]

While he was employed at the Balch Library, Ashton initiated efforts to desegregate other Loudoun County facilities, including movie theaters, bowling alleys and swimming pools. In 1963, he was arrested for sitting in the main level of the Tally-Ho Movie Theater (Black people were only allowed in the balcony seats). NAACP member Gladys Bryant Lewis secured his release. Ashton encouraged other Black youths to picket the movie theater, one of the last remaining segregated theaters in Northern Virginia, until management gave in and allowed them to sit on the main level. Ashton and his friends then turned their attention to the local bowling alley, which

Thomas Balch Library, shown here in 1949, began as a subscription library. It became public in 1960 and was integrated by 1965. *Winslow Williams Photograph Collection (VC 0003) Rust Archive, Thomas Balch Library, Leesburg, VA.*

quickly moved to admit customers of all races. But when Ashton and his friends tried the same method of protest at Leesburg Firemen's pool, the facility refused to integrate, eventually closing altogether to avoid integration. Leesburg then had no public swimming pool until the Ida Lee Recreation Center was built in 1990.[253]

Just as Thomas Balch Library had Ashton on staff before it was formally integrated, Purcellville Library also benefited from the labor of Black residents prior to integration. Reginald "Reggie" Simms mended damaged books for the library while it was segregated, as had his father before him. The irony was that his work kept books in circulation—books he was unable to check out due to his race. He remarked, "That was just natural living in the South....That's just the way it was."[254]

According to Simms, both he and his father were employed for this purpose by Gertrude Robey. Simms described her as being "a nice lady" who had some influence on his pursuit of an art career, but he expressed incredulity at her support for segregation in a video-recorded interview: "She was a suffragette—women's rights. She went to Washington, but when she came back to Purcellville…that didn't mean she wanted *me* to come and sit down at the table with her or go into the library.…She believed the races should be separate.…But that is absolutely crazy."[255]

Gertrude and her husband, Purcellville National Bank president Clarence Robey, were among the founders of the library. Gertrude was so active in library operations, she was dubbed "Mrs. Library." She even broke a leg falling off scaffolding she had climbed to inspect the library's construction. The Robeys had helped finance facilities for Black citizens, including the Willing Workers School, built by Joseph Cook and Grace Annex Methodist Church in Purcellville.[256] But they opposed integration; Mrs. Robey was among the library board members most outspoken against it.

At one of the meetings where the board discussed desegregation, Gertrude offered to match any contribution made by members of the library board to build a separate library for Black residents and to leave money in her will for this purpose. As was the case in the city of Alexandria and elsewhere, offers to fund separate public libraries for Black residents came only after lawsuits aimed at integrating the main library. But almost two decades had passed since the Alexandria Library sit-in, and Virginia's law was now clear. Loudoun's library would skip this step and move directly to full integration.

The Role of School Libraries During Segregation

Prior to Purcellville Library's existence, white residents of Loudoun had access to some private lending libraries, including a small library managed by Joseph Janney, the town's jeweler. Beginning in 1885, white residents could borrow the books housed on several shelves in Janney's shop. The service cost five cents per book or twenty-five cents per year for unlimited borrowing. The Thomas Balch Library had its roots in a small subscription library that began in 1907, which charged an annual fee of one dollar in 1917.

Prior to Purcellville Library's integration, however, the only libraries most Black Loudoun residents had access to were located in their segregated schools. Josie Cook Murray's grandfather Joseph Newton Cook, whom she was named after, helped establish one of those schools, the first school for Black children in Purcellville.[257] The Cooks' youngest daughter, Maxine, had survived scarlet fever and was unable to walk to the school that was two miles away in Lincoln. In response, Cook and his wife, Lena, founded the Willing Workers Club in 1914 with about a dozen neighbors to educate Black children close to home. Land for the school was purchased in 1917. The schoolhouse was built by Cook himself, who was a skilled stonemason and carpenter. It was opened to students in 1919.

That year, the Willing Workers Club officially incorporated "to assist in providing proper educational facilities for the colored children of Purcellville and to…equip and maintain a library and reading room for such children." To obtain books and other materials for the school library, Willing Workers borrowed $1,030 from banker Clarence Robey.[258] The school served children from grades one to six from 1919 to 1947. Willing Workers Hall, as the school was called, was deeded to the Loudoun County School Board in 1937, at which time, its name was changed to Purcellville School.

After Joseph Cook died in 1939, his widow, Lena Stewart Cook, offered seven acres of land to the Loudoun County School Board in the hopes of creating a high school for Black students. Black teenagers at that time had to travel to the Manassas Industrial School for Colored Youth to achieve a higher education—a journey that was prohibitive to most. Mrs. Cook's offer was not accepted. However, in 1945, she sold the land to the school board, and the Carver School, a school for Black children, was built there in 1947.

"We did have a good library at Carver School," recalled Harold Jackson, "And we had an excellent library and librarian [at Douglass High School in Leesburg]. And that's what took the place of not being able to go to the public library."[259] The Carver School, which operated from 1948 to 1968, was the pride of its community. The school closed after integration, and the building is now a senior center. However, the school's original library and other elements are preserved under the care of the Carver Alumni Association.[260]

While the Carver School had a spacious, well-stocked library, like those seen in public schools today, many schools at that time had tiny makeshift libraries—if they had a library at all. In *The Essence of a People*, Rosa Lee Carter describes working as a teacher for one of the poorly funded segregated schools in 1930s Loudoun.[261] Grant School in Middleburg was overcrowded, with no running water and had only a coal stove for heat. As part of her efforts to make the space cozier and more learning-friendly, Carter installed a library in one corner. It was furnished with orange crates that were painted by the children and stocked with books donated by the Community League (later the PTA). For many Black children during segregation, tiny school libraries like this would have been the extent of their library experience.

While resistance to school integration in Loudoun lingered into the 1960s, the Lincoln area of Purcellville, where the Murrays lived, had an integrated school in the 1820s. Quakers known as the Goose Creek Friends settled there in the 1700s and built a brick one-room schoolhouse, Goose Creek Friends Oakdale School, in 1815. Although the school required a small fee for enrollment, it was attended by both Black and white children.[262] It closed in 1885.

Goose Creek Friends made up much of the Community Study Group, the only integrated organization in Loudoun County. Mr. Murray was also a member. The group, which supported the desegregation of the library, later worked toward the desegregation of Loudoun County high schools.[263]

RECOGNITION

Purcellville Library, now a branch of Loudoun County Public Library, celebrated the sixtieth anniversary of the library's desegregation in 2017 with a daylong "Cross the Line" roster of events recognizing the Murrays and other civil rights activists in Loudoun. The event's activities included upholstery crafts for children. A Town of Purcellville proclamation honoring the sixtieth anniversary of the library's desegregation and the Murrays' role in achieving it is displayed in one the library's meeting rooms. It refers to the Murrays' "courage and tenacity" and reads, in part: "The Murrays' quest for equality instigated actions that ended in the first victory for the civil rights movement in Loudoun County."

In recognition of the sixtieth anniversary of Purcellville Library's desegregation, Barbara Comstock, the U.S. representative for Virginia's tenth congressional district, introduced a measure to Congress to recognize the Murrays for their contributions. "Mr. Speaker, I ask that my colleagues join me in thanking Samuel Cardoza Murray and Josie Cook Murray for their commitment to make sure that all young minds will be nurtured in our libraries, in our schools and in our homes."[264]

Purcellville Library, now a branch of Loudoun County Public Library, was founded in 1938 for white residents and was integrated in 1957. *Authors' photograph.*

The interior of Purcellville Library features original stonework. *Authors' photograph.*

Existing Sites and Landmarks

Thomas Balch Library
208 West Market Street, Leesburg, VA 20176

Thomas Balch Library began as a subscription library for white residents of Loudoun County. It became public in 1960 and was formally integrated in 1965. Today, it houses the local history and genealogy branch of the Loudoun County Public Library system.

Purcellville Library
220 East Main Street, Purcellville, VA 20132

Purcellville Library, built in 1935 and dedicated in 1938, is now part of Loudoun County Public Library. Inside, on the second floor, the original Robey Meeting Room features portraits of founders Gertrude and Clarence Robey. Across the hall, the Carruthers Room includes a portrait of librarian Jean Carruthers and a proclamation commemorating the library's desegregation.

Carver Senior Center
200 East Willie Palmer Way, Purcellville, VA 20132

Built on land once owned by the Cook family, the senior center was once the George Washington Carver School, which educated Black students through the eighth grade. The original school library is still intact inside. The school operated from 1948 until public schools fully integrated in 1968.

Goose Creek Meeting of Friends House
18204 Lincoln Road, Purcellville, VA 20132

The brick 1817 meetinghouse, originally two stories, was rebuilt as a one-story structure in 1949 due to storm damage. The stone building across the street was the original 1765 meetinghouse. Both are in the National Register of Historic Places as part of Goose Creek Historic District.

Top: Today, Thomas Balch Library houses the local history and genealogy branch of the Loudoun County Public Library system. *Authors' photograph.*

Middle: The Robey Meeting Room, Purcellville Library, features portraits of founders Gertrude and Clarence Robey. Gertrude served on the board and opposed integration in 1957. *Authors' photograph.*

Bottom: The Carruthers Room, Purcellville Library, features a portrait of long-term librarian Jean Carruthers and a framed proclamation commemorating the library's desegregation and honoring the Murrays. *Authors' photograph.*

Top: Carver Senior Center occupies the former Carver School, which was built on land once owned by the Cook family. *Authors' photograph.*

Middle: The Carver School Library is preserved within the Carver Senior Center. The library and other interior elements of the school are tended by the Carver Alumni Association. *Authors' photograph.*

Bottom: The Goose Creek Friends Meeting House dates from 1817. To the right is the former 1765 meeting house, now a caretaker's home. *Authors' photograph.*

Top: The Lyles Funeral Home occupies the original Willing Workers School. Built in 1919, the school included a library. Today, the school's bell tower is still visible on top of the funeral home. *Authors' photograph.*

Middle: The gravestone of the Cook Murray family with Mount Olive Baptist Church in the background. Josie and Samuel Murray were buried here, along with Josie's parents. *Authors' photograph.*

Bottom: The headstones that mark Samuel C. Murray and Josie C. Murray's grave sites lie side by side in the cemetery of Purcellville's Mount Olive Baptist Church on Cooksville Road. *Authors' photograph.*

Willing Workers School Bell Tower, Atop Lyle's Funeral Home
630 South Twentieth Street, Purcellville, VA 20132

The 1919 bell tower of Willing Workers School is visible on top of Lyles Funeral Home, which occupies the original structure built by Joseph Cook that included a library.

Mount Olive Baptist Church
37762 Cooksville Road, Purcellville, VA 20132

Samuel and Josie Murray were buried in the cemetery of Mount Olive Baptist Church, near where they lived and ran their upholstery shop. The upholstery shop has been torn down, but many Loudoun residents are still proud owners of furniture created by the Murrays.

PRINCE WILLIAM COUNTY

*P*rince William County was home to several public libraries prior to the establishment of the Prince William Public Libraries (PWPL) system in 1952. Two early libraries were housed in segregated schools: the white-only Ruffner School, later renamed Osbourn High School, and the Manassas Industrial School for Colored Youth. Both came into being at the turn of the twentieth century through the generous financial support of Andrew Carnegie, who, at one time, was the richest man in the world. Another public library, the Haymarket Town Library, operated in a town that had an unwritten rule forbidding Blacks to live there.

Later, other smaller public library initiatives popped up across the county. In January 1933, the Prince William Pharmacy opened a circulating library in its store and charged borrowers three cents a day.[265] The Nokesville Woman's Club managed a library during the 1940s. The Catharpin Home Demonstration Club established a public library in April 1949, and it received books from the Virginia State Library Extension Division.[266] However, most areas of Prince William County did not have any library service whatsoever.

Before the existence of PWPL and its roving bookmobile, schools were predominantly where children, both white and Black, could access a library. In 1982, Donald E. Curtis, a lifelong resident of Prince William and the former chairman of the Prince William County Historical Commission, recalled how his high school for white students was the only source for library books:

I was born and raised in rural Prince William County during a time when there were no public library facilities available. The only library I was able to use at all was a small collection of books at the old Occoquan District High School.[267]

Wilson graduated from Occoquan District High School in 1950, two years before the area's first visit from the PWPL Bookmobile and eleven years before thirteen-year-old Joyce Russell integrated the school's successor, Gar-Field Senior High School, in September 1961. Prince William County's last segregated school quietly integrated in 1966, but it was the county's first public school, a school for white children, that gave birth to Prince William's first public library.

THE RUFFNER-CARNEGIE LIBRARY

Prince William County did not embrace free public education until after the Civil War, but when it did, its public schools were formally segregated like those in the rest of Virginia. They remained segregated for nearly a century. In 1869, the newly formed Manassas School District became home to the Manassas Village White School, Prince William's first free public school. Opening in December 1869, the school met in a room of the Asbury-Methodist Episcopal Church. The following year, Prince William's second public school, the Manassas Village Colored School, was established on Liberty Street for the town's Black children.[268]

In 1872, both schools received new names. The Manassas Village Colored School became the Brown School, named in honor of the school's benefactor, Mary D. Brown, a Philadelphia Quaker. The Manassas Village White School renamed itself the Ruffner School after William Henry Ruffner, Virginia's first state superintendent of public instruction. Along with its new name, the Ruffner School expanded and moved into a new two-story structure at Center and Peabody Streets.

In 1899, the Ruffner School received a twenty-four-by-thirty-four-foot third-story addition to specifically accommodate a library. For some time, the school's principal had been soliciting books for the sole purpose of establishing a public library. William Henry Wadsworth Moran, the editor of the *Manassas Journal*; George C. Round, a Manassas District School Board member; and other citizens supported the principal's effort and convinced the Manassas District School Board to construct a third story on the Ruffner School for the library.

A postcard image of the Ruffner School's main building, erected in 1872. The Ruffner-Carnegie Library was housed on the school's third floor addition, seen here. *Authors' collection.*

Round reached out to industrialist and philanthropist Andrew Carnegie to secure funding for the library. Carnegie, who had made his fortune in the steel industry, had a passion for funding free public libraries. Known as the "patron saint of libraries," he financed the construction of 2,509 libraries around the world between 1883 and 1929—1,689 in the United States alone.[269] Carnegie's attitude concerning libraries was perfectly summed up in an article he wrote for the *North American Review*, published in December 1889:

> *No millionaire will go far wrong in his search for one of the best forms for the use of his surplus who chooses to establish a free library in any community that is willing to maintain and develop it. John Bright's words should ring in his ear: "It is impossible for any man to bestow a greater benefit upon a young man than to give him access to books in a free library."*[270]

Carnegie agreed to donate $1,000 worth of books to the Ruffner School, with the stipulation that they were to be used by the public and that the school board construct a third story for the library. The completed third floor was dedicated on January 1, 1900, and when the Ruffner-Carnegie Library opened in the space later that year, it became the first public library in Prince William County. In a December 1899 report to the county school board, the Manassas District School Board wrote:

Left: In 1899, Andrew Carnegie donated $1,000 to Ruffner School to purchase books for its library. In 1910, his donation to Manassas Industrial School for Colored Youth resulted in the construction of the Carnegie Building, which included a library. *Library of Congress*.

Below: A postcard image of Manassas High School, later renamed Osbourn High School. The school's Ruffner-Carnegie Library reopened in this space on November 10, 1927. *Authors' collection*.

The trustees wish it distinctly understood that the library is to be a circulating library, opened at stated intervals, and to be conducted according to the usual rules and regulations of public circulating libraries, for the benefit not only of those of school age but of persons of all ages.[271]

Those persons of all ages did not include Prince William County's Black population. The library's location in a white school restricted access to only white residents. It would be another decade before Black students received their own library at the Manassas Industrial School for Colored Youth, also funded by Andrew Carnegie, in 1910.

Originally, the four teachers at the Ruffner School took turns checking out and receiving library books. A designated librarian was eventually hired, and the library's operation was facilitated by high school volunteers, including during the summer months. In 1926, overcrowding at the Ruffner School required the construction of a thirteen-room brick high school building at Lee Avenue and Peabody Street. Renamed Manassas High School, the Ruffner-Carnegie Library opened in its new quarters there on Thursday, November 10, 1927. During its formal opening, the Manassas High School Community League's library committee held a "Silver Tea" benefit to raise funds for acquiring books, as the library had not been granted any kind of appropriations.[272] The Ruffner-Carnegie Library served the community as a combination public and high school library in this space for the next quarter-century.

The Manassas chapter of the United Daughters of the Confederacy (UDC) was an ardent supporter of the Ruffner-Carnegie Library. It consistently loaned or donated Confederate materials and had its own designated UDC shelf. Throughout the 1930s, the UDC sponsored library exhibits featuring books and other materials highlighting the Confederacy, typically during the week of Robert E. Lee's birthday (January 19).[273] The library grew to have a large supply of Confederate materials, as the *Manassas Journal* reported in June 1936:

This includes history, literature, economics, social studies and biography— with Douglass Freeman's great new life of Lee—as well as a long list of southern fiction....As a means of refreshing ones' memory of an historic period, there is no better way than to read a good novel vibrant with sympathy and understanding of that period, and the library patrons will find a number of these that are well worth reading.[274]

The development and growth of the library occurred under the direction of Eugenia H. Osbourn, the principal of Manassas High School from 1912 to 1935. After Osbourn's retirement, the school board appointed her the permanent librarian of the Ruffner-Carnegie Library, a role she cherished from 1935 to 1942. "Miss Eugenia was a great lover of books. Her taste in literature was truly cosmopolitan. She was an excellent book reviewer," recalled Clarence Wagener, a columnist for the *Manassas Journal*, shortly after her death.[275] In June 1938, Osbourn was the driving force behind the school's alumni organization forming a Friends of the Library group, which supported growing the library's collection.[276] The school board renamed the school Osbourn High School in her honor in 1939, and after her retirement from her position as the librarian, Osbourn continued purchasing books for the library until her death in 1951.

In addition to receiving support from the Friends of the Library and the Manassas chapter of the UDC, the Manassas Town Council, in January 1938, voted to annually appropriate one hundred dollars for acquiring books and magazines for general usage by the public.[277] This aid was supplemented with appropriations from the school board, Prince William County and the State Aid Library Fund. Additional annual contributions came from the parent-teacher association, Woman's Club of Manassas and the Manassas Kiwanis Club. The state library also loaned one hundred fiction and nonfiction books to the library on a quarterly basis.

Despite the widespread support from the residents, town, county and state, the Ruffner-Carnegie Library continued to remain inaccessible to Prince William County's Black residents throughout its existence. When the Extension Division of the Virginia State Library published its *Statistics of Virginia Public Libraries* in 1945 and 1946, which included "Service to Negroes" data, the Ruffner-Carnegie Library did not fall within this category. It was not until 1965, when Osbourn High School desegregated, that the library became accessible to students of all races.

By then, Osbourn High School was housed in a new building that had opened in 1953. The school's library had dropped the Ruffner-Carnegie name after the move, but it did remain publicly open to white residents as late as 1957, along with the school libraries in Brentsville District High School and Gar-Field High School.[278] It is unclear when the library ceased being a dual public and high school library, but today, PWPL's local history and genealogy room, the Ruth E. Lloyd Information Center (RELIC), preserves several books from the Ruffner-Carnegie Library in its rare book cabinet.

MANASSAS INDUSTRIAL SCHOOL
FOR COLORED YOUTH LIBRARY

Just a short distance south from the Ruffner School and across the Southern Railway tracks was the Manassas Industrial School for Colored Youth. Founded in 1893 by Jane Serepta "Jennie" Dean (1848–1913), the training school served thousands of Black children who attended from across Northern Virginia. Dean, who was born into slavery in Prince William County, worked as a domestic servant in Washington for a time and established several Sunday schools and churches in the area following her emancipation after the Civil War. Dean's experience in missionary work inspired her to build a training school that would teach Black children skilled trades to earn a useful living. She recalled in 1906:

> *One October morning, a farmer called to see me about his children. He had seven sons and he wanted them to have trades. Time passed on, and at length, one cold January morning in 1888, my mother, Reverend D.G. Henderson and I were sitting by a log fire, talking over the condition and welfare of the young colored people. I had found through the Sunday school work that many of the boys and girls would be smart in more ways than one if they had an opportunity. I had begun to think what could be done for them. I planned in my mind a long time. The farmer and his seven sons made it clear what kind of a school we needed. I told what I had in mind, what kind of teachers we needed and how to get food and other necessary things to begin with.*[279]

Dean spent the next three years embarking on an aggressive fundraising campaign both locally and in the North to make the school a reality. She succeeded in convincing several influential men and women, both white and Black, to donate to the cause. Additionally, she spent many hours on the road with her mule Chaney, making house visits to inspire interest in local Black families who wanted a better future for their children.[280] Through donations, she was able to secure a 125-acre farm three miles from the town of Manassas as a site for the school. In October 1893, the Manassas Industrial School for Colored Youth received its charter, and it was dedicated in a ceremony on September 3, 1894.[281]

The keynote speaker for the event was noted abolitionist Frederick Douglass. The ceremony occurred on the fifty-sixth anniversary of his escape from slavery. He was quick to note the significance of a school

Left: Jennie Dean in 1893. Born enslaved in Prince William County, she founded the Manassas Industrial School for Colored Youth. *Manassas Museum System, Manassas, Virginia.*

Right: Frederick Douglass, circa 1881. He was the keynote speaker at the dedication ceremony for the Manassas Industrial School for Colored Youth on September 3, 1894. *Library of Congress.*

being built for Black children on the first battlefield of the Civil War, where just thirty years prior, the Union and Confederate armies fought over the question of the perpetual enslavement of Black Americans. "We are to witness here a display of the best elements of advanced civilization and good citizenship," said Douglass during the dedication. "It is to be the place where the children of a once-enslaved people may realize the blessings of liberty and education and learn how to make for themselves, and for all others, the best of both worlds."[282]

From its inception, the Manassas Industrial School was the only high school for Black children in Northern Virginia. Students began attending classes the following month inside a preexisting house on the property. In time, additional school buildings were constructed on the campus using donated funds, and the school grew into a flourishing farm of workshops, dairies and poultry yards.[283] The campus saw its share of tragedy when fires destroyed school buildings in 1895 and 1900, but they were promptly rebuilt.

The Manassas Industrial School was open to both boys and girls on equal terms. In addition to the Northern Virginia region, students came from

Washington, D.C., and ten other states throughout its operation. The school charged tuition fees, which varied over the years, but it ultimately relied on donations as a source of income. The school's curriculum comprised liberal arts courses and training in blacksmithing, carpentry, shoe repair, farming and wheelwrighting for boys. Girls received instruction in sewing, dressmaking, cooking, childcare and laundry work, among other trades.

Over the next decade, the school received contributions from donors, both rich and poor, white and Black, including many famous twentieth-century individuals, such as Thomas Edison, Frances (Mrs. J.P.) Morgan and Andrew Carnegie.[284] Carnegie, who had funded Manassas's Ruffner-Carnegie Library into existence in 1899, became a regular benefactor of the Manassas Industrial School. In 1905, the school offered its presidency to Oswald Garrison Villard, the editor of the *New York Evening Post* and a white founding member of the NAACP. Villard accepted the position and wrote in his acceptance letter, "Perhaps you have already heard that my taking the presidency has had a pleasant omen in the receipt by me of a check for $1,000, which I received from Mr. [Andrew] Carnegie on Saturday. He has told me since then that 'we must hold up that woman's hands at any cost. She must not be allowed to go down.'" This was in reference to Jennie Dean, who had continued to be the school's superintendent.[285]

By 1910, Carnegie donated $15,000 to cover one-half of the construction of an administration building with a library and classrooms. The remainder of the money was raised by both white and Black donors. Upon its completion, the handsome three-story building consisted of a library and school administration offices on the first floor, classrooms on the second and an assembly hall on the third floor. Initially known as the Library and Trades Building, it was later renamed the Carnegie Building in honor of the school's benefactor. It held its grand opening in January 1911.[286]

Having a library at the school was of national significance. In 1916, the Department of the Interior's Bureau of Education published a bulletin titled *Negro Education: A Study of the Private and Higher Schools for Colored People in the United States*. It stated, "Library facilities for Negroes in the southern states are very inadequate." Out of the 653 private and higher-learning schools listed in the report, only 27 were known to have a library, which included the Manassas Industrial School. Until then, the Carnegie Corporation of New York is mentioned in the report as having financed the construction of sixteen libraries for Black students. The Manassas Industrial School, being one of them, was the only such library funded in Virginia.[287]

The Carnegie Building, seen here in the 1950s, housed a library on the first floor. *Manassas Museum System, Manassas, Virginia.*

The report drove home the importance of donors to the private school's continued success. At the time, the state supported only a single institution of higher education for Black students—Virginia Union University in Richmond. The commonwealth also had only six publicly funded high schools and twenty-three private schools.[288] Securing financial support became increasingly difficult over the ensuing years, and the Manassas Industrial School eventually fell into sizeable debt.

Although her direct influence over the school's operations waned with time, Jennie Dean remained interested and involved with the school until her death in 1913. In 1938, the counties of Fairfax, Fauquier and Prince William agreed to purchase the Manassas Industrial School, which had been troubled with debt and depreciation. Those counties' school boards acquired the campus for use as a regional public high school. Consequently, many students spent hours commuting on buses to receive an education at Regional High School. Some students would stay in the dormitories on the campus and return home on the weekends.

Regional High School students continued using the Carnegie Building library and formed a library club, which was responsible for maintaining and expanding the library's collection for the duration of the school's existence. The Prince William County School Board also approved appropriations to support the library beginning in the early 1940s. Unlike the white-only

Ruffner-Carnegie Library, surviving records have not confirmed whether the Carnegie Building library ever served as a dual public library for Prince William County's Black residents. However, there was another institution in the county that attempted to fill that role.

In March 1940, the school board began funding an already existing "Negro County Wide Circulating Library." Little is known about this initiative or how it got started. Five years later, in February 1945, the Prince William County Negro County-Wide League asked the school board to make an appropriation to assist community activist Adeline Penn, a Black maid, in her work with the Negro County-Wide Library. Each of the Black schools had raised a total of twenty dollars to aid her efforts, and the school board unanimously agreed to contribute an additional twenty-five dollars.[289] Eight months later, the library was reportedly housed in such poor conditions that the school board authorized Superintendent Richard C. Haydon to find a better location, with the rental fee not to exceed ninety dollars.[290] The library's fate and how effective it truly was currently remains unknown and requires additional research.

Students study inside the Carnegie Library of the Regional High School (formerly Manassas Industrial School for Colored Youth), circa 1950–52. *Manassas Museum System, Manassas, Virginia.*

In 1954, most of the Northern Virginia counties that bused their students to Regional High School had those students withdrawn and placed into newly constructed all-Black high schools within their own school districts. Prince William and Warren Counties were the last to send their students to Regional High School, until 1959. That fall, Prince William County opened the new all-Black Jennie Dean High and Elementary School directly behind the old Regional High School's campus. It would remain segregated until integration in 1966.

Haymarket Town Library

Ten miles northwest of the Manassas Industrial School site lies the town of Haymarket. Chartered in 1799, the town was incorporated by an Act of Assembly in February 1882. Although not explicitly written in an ordinance, its residents had an understanding that Black people were not permitted to live in the town. Their place was restricted to the "Settlement," a thriving Black community that had been settled by freedmen following the Civil War, just south of the town's limits.[291] The 1930 and 1940 U.S. federal censuses substantiate this, showing that less than six people of color lived in Haymarket during those two decades, and all of them were either hired servants or their children.

A year after incorporating, the town raised funds to build a combined new white school and town meeting hall. At some point after the building's completion in 1883, the town council permitted the Haymarket Library Association to use a room in the building for a library. Lillian Lightner Norman, a white resident, recalled in 1985:

> *One wonderful asset was the "town library" books in the upstairs room. Several hundred books—mostly fiction—were on shelves along the wall. I think the summer people had given them. Many people from the city came to escape the heat and were a valuable asset to the community.[292]*

The library, accessible to only the town's white residents, was subscription-based, and it charged its members an annual fee of one dollar. It closed during World War I, when many of its members were involved in Red Cross work, but reopened again in August 1921 with limited morning hours on Wednesdays and Saturdays.[293] The town library temporarily closed again in January 1923 to accommodate a large enrollment of white children at the Haymarket School.[294]

The Haymarket Town Library was located on the second floor of this building. Today, it is the Haymarket Museum. *Authors' photograph.*

The library eventually reopened again, and in 1931, it came under the auspices of the newly formed Woman's Club of Haymarket, which used the library as its headquarters.[295] It painted and renovated the town library and maintained it well into the 1940s. By 1954, the women had converted the space into a club room. The library's successor, PWPL's Gainesville-Haymarket Library, opened to everyone in a brand-new building a mile north of the town's limits in October 2015.

Prince William Public Libraries (PWPL)

A fully fledged county public library accessible to all citizens had been a long time coming for Prince William County. On July 18, 1947, Rosamond B. Hanson, the editor of the *Manassas Messenger*, wrote in an editorial:

> *The Ruffner-Carnegie Library is not a county library of the kind we ought to have. It is not even adequate as a library for Manassas District or the town of Manassas. But in our opinion, it has done a wonderful job with the scant funds at its disposal.*[296]

Prince William County Public Library's first bookmobile, 1953. *Ruth E. Lloyd Information Center (RELIC), Prince William Public Libraries.*

The Woman's Club of Manassas had long supported the white-only Ruffner-Carnegie Library. They gave annual contributions for the purchase of library books and often gifted new volumes. In 1939, it organized a reading circle that met twice a month in the library, where members discussed literature and reviewed books. The club also sponsored the library's book review contests for the W.C. Wagener Memorial Prize. Aware of the Ruffner-Carnegie Library's limitations, in June 1951, the women's club began investigating what could be done to improve it. Through the persistence of the chairman of the club's library committee Ruth Emmons Lloyd (1892–1971), the group successfully petitioned for a new state-funded demonstration public library.

The club invited Ernestine Grafton, the head of the Extension Division of the Virginia State Library, to speak at its meeting on Monday, October 22, 1951, in Trinity Episcopal Church's parish hall.[297] Grafton provided information about the state library's bookmobile project, and in November, the women voted that a campaign for a county library would be their project of the year.[298] The drive for a library quickly took off and generated tremendous enthusiasm within the community. Posters, window displays and hundreds of letters were written to the Prince William County Board of Supervisors, petitioning for library service. The campaign was led by two segregated committees. Ruth E. Lloyd served as chairman of the county library committee, and a Mrs. Barnes chaired the "negro county committee."[299]

The following January, Grafton wrote to Ruth Ashburn, the librarian of Fairfax County Public Library (FCPL), requesting permission that the library's bookmobile be exhibited in Manassas at a meeting of citizens interested in establishing a county library. At the time, the FCPL Bookmobile was the only vehicle of its kind in Northern Virginia. Its exhibition at the Prince William library campaign rally on January 24, 1952, caused considerable interest among the residents of Manassas.[300]

Consequently, Prince William became the first county in Virginia selected for a public library demonstration project funded by new state aid laws passed by the Virginia General Assembly. Under the program, the state library's Extension Division purchased a book collection, furniture, supplies and a bookmobile for Prince William County. At the conclusion of the one-year demonstration period, everything would be turned over to a county-appointed library board if the county government appropriated funds for its continuous operation. The Prince William County Board of Supervisors agreed to the terms and supported the state's library project with a small expenditure on April 17, 1952.[301]

The women's club secured a twenty-by-twenty-foot storage room off an alley behind the Martha Shop at 110½ North Main Street in the town of Manassas for use as the demonstration library. It directed the remodeling efforts with assistance from the Chamber of Commerce, Kiwanis, Lions Club and Home Demonstration Club. Men from the Church of the Brethren's Cannon Branch installed a new ceiling and shelving in the former storage room, while the woman's club focused on redecorating the interior. It hung up a map that featured the bookmobile's route and a portrait of former Ruffner-Carnegie librarian Eugenia Osbourn, to whom the club dedicated the space.[302] The county agreed to pay $500 for the building's rent and utilities.

On May 29, 1952, Worth H. Storke, the county clerk, swore in the Prince William County Public Library Demonstration Advisory Committee at its first meeting. Its members included Ruth E. Lloyd; Lillian Carden; Audrey Kerr; Supervisor J. Carl Kincheloe; J.A. Garber, the superintendent of Prince William County Public Schools; and Ernestine Grafton, the head of the Extension Division of the Virginia State Library. The committee would continue without Grafton as the official library board after the demonstration period ended and the library was turned over to the county. Ruth E. Lloyd was appointed chairman at the meeting, a position she held until she retired in July 1958.

The interior of the Prince William County Public Library Demonstration Project behind the Martha Shop in Manassas. *Ruth E. Lloyd Information Center (RELIC), Prince William Public Libraries.*

During the same meeting, Ernestine Grafton suggested several publicity ideas to the committee. She recommended holding a bookmobile schedule hearing for all interested citizens in the county, and this occurred at the Prince William County Courthouse on June 27, 1952.[303] She also urged for announcements about the library's opening to be sent out to every household and said that bookmobile schedules should be mailed to every rural residence. Additionally, she called for hosting "special programs with the Negro organizations, emphasizing the special Negro book collection in the county library."[304] This statement, recorded in the meeting's minutes, could be interpreted as there possibly being a segregated book collection; however, no policies or discussions ever hint at discrimination in the library board's minutes. The library and its collection were ostensibly open to everyone from their inception.

The Prince William County Library officially opened in an elaborate ceremony on Wednesday, July 16, 1952, at 7:30 p.m. An enthusiastic crowd braved showers to examine the library's headquarters and the cream-and-green Boyertown Chevrolet bookmobile, which had room for over two thousand books. During the ceremony, County Librarian Margie Malmberg gave a speech saying that all library books, magazines and records were available to everyone, and she encouraged the community to take advantage of both the Headquarters Library and its bookmobile.[305]

When it opened, the library contained 3,500 books and a robust reference collection that included *Who's Who in Colored America*. Mary Anne Peters, a voluntary publicity director for the library, wrote a weekly newspaper column titled "Our County Library" for the *Manassas Journal Messenger*. In the editorial, she wrote of new titles available at the library and provided book recommendations. In recognition of "National Negro Week" in 1954, she spotlighted many of the library's books pertaining to Black leaders and novelists. Some of the titles included *The Story of Phyllis Wheatley*, *There Once Was a Slave: The Heroic Story of Frederick Douglas* and *Marian Anderson, a Portrait*.[306]

According to Donald L. Wilson, Virginiana librarian for the Ruth E. Lloyd Information Center (RELIC), the Black community may not have felt entirely comfortable visiting the library:

> *A few years ago, I asked Ren Conner, son of one of the earliest staff, Katherine Conner [1910–2005], if the library was segregated. His mother was acting library director during several periods in the 1950s and 1960s. Ren said that on his many visits to our library, he never saw a person of color using it. He consulted some friends whose memory also went back that far, and they agreed with his assessment.*[307]

While there may have been limitations in terms of accessibility and feeling welcome, PWPL did include service to Black residents from the beginning. As early as 1953, the bookmobile visited Black neighborhoods and allowed children inside to browse the collection on their own, something that Fairfax County Public Library's bookmobile did not permit during its earliest years. Some Black communities that the PWPL bookmobile scheduled stops at during its inaugural year included Mount Zion Baptist Church in Joplin, Howard William's Store in Agnewville and Jacob's Corner in Antioch.[308]

PWPL also built a working relationship with the county's school system. The bookmobile began serving public schools in October 1952. During its first year of operations, the bookmobile's weekly schedule included visits to both Black and white schools on the same day. The all-Black schools that were visited included Antioch School, Brown School, Macrae School, Washington-Reid Elementary School and the Regional High School.[309] Although the bookmobile's route and schedule changed over the next

Prince William County Public Library's bookmobile at Russell's Store in Canova. *Ruth E. Lloyd Information Center (RELIC), Prince William Public Libraries.*

decade, it continued to visit most of these schools well into the early 1960s, before they were desegregated.

Zella Brown, one of the four Black teachers chosen to integrate Prince William County Public Schools in 1966, originally taught at the all-Black Antioch-McRae Elementary School in Haymarket, which opened in 1953. On March 26, 2022, she recalled the bookmobile visiting her school at the seventh annual Prince William/Manassas History Symposium held at the Old Manassas Courthouse:

> *At Antioch-McRae, there was no library. There was a bookmobile. The bookmobile was like a big van or whatever, and it would come around to the schools. Children were allowed to go in there and look and see if there was a book that they would like to take out, and they would return it to the bookmobile when it came back around. So, that's what was going on in the Black schools. We didn't have a library. Now, there was one in the white school—a library, a nice one.*[310]

During the same panel session, RELIC Room librarian Donald Wilson asked Brown what her experiences were using the original Headquarters Library:

> *Wilson: At that time, there was only one public library building in the county in Manassas. Did you feel comfortable visiting it or using its services?*

Children using the Prince William County Public Library's bookmobile in the 1950s. *Ruth E. Lloyd Information Center (RELIC), Prince William Public Libraries.*

Brown: It was OK. You know, I was curious, and I thought I would like visiting the library for different reasons. As time went on, things got better, and I felt more comfortable and I would go more often. So, it just progressed from one level to the other.

Wilson: But you were not refused service there?

Brown: No. I don't recall that, no.[311]

During Book Week in November 1953, the library featured a display of new juvenile and adult books. The Brown School, Prince William County's first public school established for Black children in 1870, was invited to the library for class visits. The December 8, 1953 library board minutes recorded that "grades five and six with Mrs. [Louise Smith] Brown and grades six and seven with Miss Scott" made class visits to the library.[312] The Brown School permanently closed the following year.

PWPL also built a rapport with the Regional High School. In May 1953, the library exhibited oil paintings of two of the school's Black students. Aaron Betz of Mount Pleasant in Alexandria and Clyde Smith of Merrifield each had four of their paintings put on display at the library headquarters on Main Street. The paintings had been entered in the Virginia State Art Contest at Virginia State College earlier that year, and judges selected Betz's painting *Christ* as the alternate for the first-place scholarship.[313]

"I didn't even know they were on display there," remarked an eighty-seven-year-old Betz in May 2022. "It's a surprise to me because I never got them back. I've stayed in touch with Clyde, and I always thought the pictures were stolen." During the 1953–54 school year, Betz served as president and Clyde as vice-president of the Regional High School's library club in the Carnegie Building. Betz could not remember if the school's library was publicly open during his time there but recalled that the curriculum required students to go to the library during a certain hour. "I was in the library a lot to do sketching," he recalled. Betz went on to have a lifelong career in commercial art and continues to paint to this day. "I was really proud of that school," he said.[314] The current whereabouts of the paintings remain unknown. They were never returned to Betz or Clyde after the exhibition.

Two years later, in 1955, the Regional High School invited librarian Marion L. Robertson and her assistant, Mrs. Robert F. Powell, to come and speak at a school meeting of teachers. They discussed bookmobile service to the school and the library's available reference books. Later that year, the *Manassas Journal Messenger* reported:

> *The teachers of Regional High and Elementary visited the library recently to orient themselves with the library and its facilities. The library welcomes opportunities to assist teachers and schools in any way and was pleased to have these teachers visit the library en masse.*[315]

On July 16, 1953, the county's Board of Supervisors officially accepted the Prince William County Library demonstration project from the state, and the library and bookmobile were turned over during a special ceremony at the courthouse. PWPL suffered the same fate as all Northern Virginia public libraries in this era: crowded conditions and a lack of funding. The library moved into Edith Fitzwater's former beauty shop at the corner of Church and Main Streets in 1955, and it moved again, in May 1960, to the old Reassessment Building at 221 Peabody Street. It moved a third time, in September 1962, to the old Board of Supervisors' chambers in the Law Building on Lee Avenue.[316]

It was in this location that, in August 1964, the Manassas chapter of the UDC loaned a collection of books about the Confederacy to the library to be housed on a special shelf. This tradition appears to have carried over from the days when the organization loaned and purchased similar materials for the Ruffner-Carnegie Library. The loan was made in memory of the group's longtime president Isabelle Hutchison of Manassas.[317] Except for three volumes, the UDC withdrew the books in December 1965 and gave them to the reference collection at the Manassas National Battlefield Park.[318]

PWPL expanded its services when its first branch, named Leesylvania, opened in Woodbridge with three thousand books in September 1965.[319] A permanent Central Library was finally built and dedicated on Mathis Avenue in Manassas on January 30, 1971.[320] A plaque affixed in the building's lobby dedicated the library "to all citizens for a happier-richer-better informed life." Today, PWPL maintains twelve physical branches throughout the county and the city of Manassas. They are open and accessible to everyone.

RECOGNITION

The Carnegie Building and other buildings of the Manassas Industrial School for Colored Youth campus were demolished in the late 1960s. However, the site of the school is now a memorial. A six-foot-tall bronze statue of Jennie Dean, created by artist Chris Hill, stands there today. It was unveiled on October 24, 2020, at an event emceed by Manassas Mayor Hal Parris, with speakers including Virginia Lieutenant Governor Justin Fairfax, Senator Mark Warner and Representative Jennifer Wexton (D-10).[321] It is one of only 3 percent of public outdoor statues in the U.S. that depict a woman of color.[322] Jennie Dean Elementary School, located at 9601 Prince William Street in Manassas, overlooks the memorial. The school's students are known as the Jennie Dean Dolphins.

At the Jennie Dean Memorial in Manassas, a statue of Dean appears to gesture toward the arch of the Carnegie Building, which housed the school's library. *Authors' photograph.*

Existing Sites and Landmarks

The Site of Ruffner-Carnegie Library (1900–1926)
Center Street, West of Peabody Street, Manassas, VA 20110

The Ruffner School, built in 1872, had a third-floor addition built specifically to house a public library. Funded by Andrew Carnegie, the Ruffner-Carnegie Library served the community as a combination public and school library until it was moved into the new Manassas High School in 1927. The building was demolished in 1930, and an elm tree was planted in its place.[323] A state historical marker commemorating the school was erected in 1965.

The Site of Carnegie Building Library at Manassas Industrial School
for Colored Youth (1911–1959)
9601 Prince William Street, Manassas, VA 20110

Along with a six-foot-tall bronze statue of Dean, the Jennie Dean Memorial site includes a recreated arch of the Carnegie Building, the footprints and cornerstones of original buildings, a bronze scale model of the campus, historical markers and interpretive signage. The grounds were listed in the National Register of Historic Places in 1994, and the five-acre memorial was dedicated as an archaeological site in 1995. The Manassas Museum organizes guided tours of the site.

A sign facing the road marks the location of the Jennie Dean Memorial Site, where the Manassas Industrial School for Colored Youth was founded in 1893. *Authors' photograph.*

The recreated arch and footprint of the Carnegie Building. *Authors' photograph.*

Haymarket Museum, the Site of Haymarket Town Library (circa 1912–the late 1940s) 15025 Washington Street, Haymarket, VA 20169

The Haymarket Town Library was located on the second floor of this building for many years. The building continued to be used as a community meeting place until an electrical fire damaged the interior in 2001. The building was renovated and reopened as the Haymarket Museum in September 2002. The former library space is now used for museum storage and as an office.

Part II

"We Stand on the Threshold"

Elsewhere in Virginia and Washington, D.C.

NOTABLE CASES ELSEWHERE
IN VIRGINIA

Segregation as a part of the fabric of American life is dead.
We stand on the threshold of America becoming her ideal.
—C.J. Malloy

Although the Southeastern Library Association recommended in 1928 that "library service to Negroes should be a part of every public library program," as of 1939, only 21 percent of the Black population in the thirteen southern states were provided with public library service.[324] A 1935 survey published by Louis Round Wilson, President of the American Library Association (ALA), showed that of the forty-six public libraries in Virginia, only eight served Black residents.[325]

Statistics of Virginia Public Libraries 1944–45 lists eighty-six public libraries in the state, and reports that thirteen provided "service to Negroes" in the main library, while fifteen had a separate branch to serve Black residents. In two cases, the same library system reported it provided service to Black residents in both its main library and a separate branch, which amounts to twenty-six separate library systems out of the eighty-six that provided some sort of service to Black residents.

The counties of Danville, Newport News, Petersburg and Portsmouth were the sites of well-publicized library desegregation cases elsewhere in Virginia during the 1950s and 1960s. Following are brief descriptions of each of those cases.

DANVILLE

The Danville Public Library was also known as Confederate Memorial Library, because it resided in the 1859 Sutherlin Mansion that was used by Jefferson Davis to hold his last cabinet meeting of the Civil War. Danville itself is sometimes known as the "last capital of the Confederacy" because of the events that took place in the mansion during the week leading up to Robert E. Lee's surrender on April 10, 1865. The home later became a public library, opening in 1928 for use by white residents only.

Although the library was segregated, in the early 1930s, a Black assistant named Frankie H. Jones was hired by the white librarian and sometimes took over duties when the white librarian was absent. Later, a branch opened at the high school for Black students, and Jones was transferred there. In 1950, a library branch for Black residents opened and was named William F. Grasty Library after a local Black educator.[326] As was usually the case, the library designated for Black residents was much smaller than one designated for white residents and contained older books that had been discarded from the main library.[327] While officials claimed Black residents had equal access to materials from either library, there was no access to the catalogue from Grasty Library.

On April 2, 1960, a group of Black teenagers, led by seventeen-year-old high school student Robert A. Williams, protested the segregated facilities by "invading" the white-only library. They were not allowed to check out books and were told the library was closed. The teenagers, who knew each other from high school and Loyal Baptist Church, also protested a segregated park. A week later, crosses were burned on the lawn of the Loyal Baptist Church. On September 4, while the library remained closed as officials attempted to forestall integration, the KKK gathered at a racetrack nearby for a speech given by its imperial wizard. The group burned a cross and raised the Confederate flag. However, continued civil rights protests and legal action compelled the city council to vote on September 13, 1960, to integrate the library.

When the Danville Public Library reopened as an integrated facility, there were new requirements in place, including a four-page library card application and a $2.50 membership fee. The cumbersome application required users to list their education level, college degrees, reasons for using the library, reading habits, et cetera. Applicants were also required to supply two character and two credit references, which local officials promised to review with "rigid scrutiny."[328] Also upon reopening, the library's furniture had been removed to require standing-only service, as that was thought to

Confederate Memorial Library, Danville, Virginia

A postcard of Danville Public Library, also known as Confederate Memorial Library and the Sutherlin Mansion. Today, the building houses the Danville Museum of Fine Arts and History. *Authors' collection.*

be less "intimate" than having people of different races seated together. Clearly, although residents of all races were allowed to enter the library, the environment was not a welcoming one.

EXISTING SITES AND LANDMARKS

Danville Museum of Fine Arts and History (Formerly Danville Public Library) 975 Main Street, Danville, Virginia 24541

Originally the Sutherlin Mansion, built in 1859 for Major William T. Sutherlin, the house was the temporary residence (April 3–10, 1865) of Confederate president Jefferson Davis until the news of Lee's surrender reached him. It later became the site of the white-only Danville Public Library, also known as the Confederate Memorial Library, until activists succeeded in integrating the library in 1960. Today, the mansion houses exhibits, including one outlining the timeline of the Danville civil rights movement.

The Site of William F. Grasty Library
320 Holbrook Street, Danville, VA, 24541

On Friday, July 30, 2021, a historical marker was dedicated, commemorating the history of the Mary B. Yancey House and Grasty Library. The Yancey House was a lodging place for Black Americans during segregation. The Grasty Library was a segregated library for Black residents prior to desegregation of the Danville Public Library. The Grasty Library, which once stood next door to the Yancey House, has since been torn down.

NEWPORT NEWS

In Newport News, W. Hale Thompson (1914–1966), who was a local attorney and vice chairman of the Virginia NAACP's legal staff, sued the city and the library board in 1950 for access to the public library on West Avenue. A trial date was set in 1952, but before that time, the library system announced its facilities were open to "all adult inhabitants of the city of Newport News," apparently due to pressure from the lawsuit. While some claim that Newport News was the first county in Virginia to desegregate a formerly segregated public library, Arlington Public Library preceded Newport News in doing so by two years. However, Newport News was the first to desegregate as the result of legal action by a citizen.

Even before the 1950 lawsuit, however, Thompson had been lobbying for library services for all residents and prompted the opening of a library for Black citizens on the second floor of the Doris Miller Recreation Building in 1949. This was a segregated facility for Black residents, and it was located two blocks from the World War II Recreation Building for white residents. Known as Branch No. 1, it was the only library available to Black children and teens after school hours, because even after the West Avenue branch integrated in 1952, it was only for adults. After moving a few times, the library morphed into the Pearl Bailey Library on Wickham Avenue in 1985.

Perhaps Thompson received some inspiration from his excellent high school library. Huntington High School, which, for a time, was the only high school for Black students in Newport News (later one of two), boasted one of the best school libraries in the state and was the only one with a full-time professional librarian. According to *Huntington High School: Symbol of Community Hope and Unity 1920–1971*, "In 1938, the Huntington High

School library was recognized and considered by some critics as one of the best in any Virginia high schools. It housed more than 3,500 books; held subscriptions to 36 then-current magazines and 6 daily newspapers, including the *Journal* and *Guide* and the *New York Times*. It was the only high school library in Virginia with a full-time librarian who had a collegiate professional degree in library science."[329] Once slated for demolition, the historic building was saved by preservation-minded community members; it is now a Boys and Girls Club.[330]

Existing Sites and Landmarks

Huntington High School
629 Hampton Avenue, Newport News, VA 23607

Now a Boys and Girls Club, Huntington High School featured a state-of-the-art library. W. Hale Thompson was a graduate. The exterior features a Black history mural by artist S. Ross Browne.

Huntington High School had a library recognized in 1938 as the only school library in Virginia with a full-time professional librarian. *Authors' photograph.*

Pearl Bailey Library
2510 Wickham Avenue, Newport News, VA 23607

This branch's history stretches back to a 1949 library on the second floor of the Doris Miller Recreation Building, founded in part in response to attorney W. Hale Thompson's attempt to desegregate the West Avenue Library. In 1985, Newport News Public Library opened Pearl Bailey Library at its present location.

Above: Pearl Bailey Library features a community room named after W. Hale Thompson. The first public library for Black residents of Newport News evolved into this branch. *Authors' photograph.*

Left: A mural of Pearl Bailey by artist Asa Jackson adorns the side of the library named in her honor. *Authors' photograph.*

Mural of W. Hale Thompson at the Site of His Former Law Office
611 Twenty-Fifth Street, Newport News, VA 23605

In 2018, artwork bearing the likeness of W. Hale Thompson was unveiled in honor of his civil rights activism. It stands on the side of the building that was once the site of Thompson's law office and is now Esquire Barber Shop. The artwork was created by local artist Asa Jackson.

Top: Signage describes "a life of accomplishment" at the site of W. Hale Thompson's former law office in Newport News. *Authors' photograph.*

Bottom: W. Hale Thompson is featured in a mural on the side of his former law office, now a barbershop. Artwork by Asa Jackson, Newport News. *Authors' photograph.*

PETERSBURG

In 1923, Clara McKenney donated her historic 1890 mansion to the City of Petersburg for use as a public library in memory of her late husband, attorney William R. McKenney. Her deed stipulated: "[The library is] to be maintained for both white and colored persons, all of the building, including the first floor and all above that was to be for the exclusive use of white persons; and the basement of the building was to be kept and maintained for the exclusive use of colored persons, with separate entrance and exit thereto."[331] The library remained segregated in this manner for decades. While all users theoretically had access to all books by request, the catalogue was in the white-only part of the library, thwarting Black users from knowing what was purportedly available to them. Reference books and current periodicals were also in the white-only part of the library.

Reverend Wyatt T. Walker (1929–2018), the pastor of Gillfield Baptist Church and president of the local chapter of NAACP, initiated change in June 1959, when he deliberately entered the white-only floor and, conspicuously wearing his clerical collar (which he did not typically wear), requested a particular biography of Robert E. Lee. He was refused service and was told to go to the basement via the separate entrance for Black customers. Walker had anticipated this and tipped off reporters.

Virginia Claiborne, the daughter of Clara McKenney, wrote to the mayor in support of integration: "The present branch facilities…represented human dignity in 1923. The same is not true in 1959."[332] Both Claiborne and Louis Brownlow, who had been city manager at the time the building was gifted, wrote letters testifying that the donor would have wanted the library to be integrated. Some other white residents also backed integration. But local segregationists insisted the gift's language meant the library could not integrate and must close if it was forced to do so.

Plans for a protest ensued, led by Reverend R.G. Williams of Zion Baptist Church, in addition to Reverend Walker and local students. Ernest Shaw (1937–2020), then a recent graduate of Virginia State University, assisted with preparations:

> *We were practicing before we could participate, for we had people with high temper. If you wanted to go out there and participate, there were some tests you had to pass. There were certain things we had to take. Maybe someone might spit on you or blow smoke in your eye. They would cuss us out. We did that in the meetings, and if you couldn't take those things, you couldn't face the public.*[333]

On February 27, 1960, approximately 140 Black residents, most of them students from Peabody High School and Virginia State College, entered the library via the main door and took all the available seats. This deliberate "trespassing" in the white-only part of the library resulted in the library closing for the next four days while the city council worked to pass a tougher ordinance to deter integration efforts.

C.J. Malloy, a twenty-year-old student at Virginia State College and one of the protesters, read a group statement at a city council meeting on March 1, 1960, while the library remained closed to avoid integration attempts. Part of the statement read: "Segregation as a part of the fabric of American life is dead. We stand on the threshold of America becoming her ideal."[334]

On March 7, 1960, fifteen Black residents again walked through the entrance reserved for white customers and took seats inside. Eleven were arrested, and due to the newly passed city ordinance, each faced up to a year in jail and a fine of up to $1,000. Five remained in jail for over forty hours and received a telegram of support from Dr. Martin Luther King Jr.

Among the protesters was Theresa Ann Walker (born in 1928), Reverend Walker's wife, who attended the protest with their children and those of another protester. When the city manager asked her to leave, adding that her refusal could lead to arrest, she responded, "I know that, and I have come prepared."[335] The city manager capitulated, saying he would not humiliate the children by having her arrested.[336]

Although informed by Police Chief W.E. Traylor that supporters had offered to bail them out, Revered Walker and several others chose to stay in jail overnight to call attention to the injustice of segregation. Reverend Milton Reid led a prayer vigil on the courthouse steps, and it was attended by two hundred citizens in support of the jailed protesters. City officials ordered the floodlights, which usually illuminated the courthouse area, be turned off during the vigil. Supporters had come prepared with flashlights.

During the vigils held while protesters remained in jail, Virginia State College student E.J. McLaughlin read a statement to the media: "Under a government which imprisons men unjustly, the true place for a just man is in prison. We did not break the law in a spirit of malice or defiance, we broke the law because we were compelled by conviction and principle."[337]

The library sit-ins inspired further protests throughout the city. Although it was compelled to desegregate in time for a May 5 visit from the Freedom Riders, the library closed again for several months before permanently reopening as an integrated facility in November 1960. Following his

Left: Virginia State College student Lillian Pride is served a warrant by Petersburg police chief W.E. Traylor on March 7, 1960. © *1960* Richmond-Times Dispatch.

Below: Sergeant A.V. Bowen tells Peabody High School students Leonard Walker (*left*) and Horace Brooks (*right*) that they are trespassing during the Petersburg Library sit-in. They were arrested for their participation. © *1960* Richmond-Times Dispatch.

Citizens gather at Petersburg Courthouse in a vigil to protest the arrest of library sit-in participants on March 8, 1960. © *1960* Richmond-Times Dispatch.

leadership of the sit-ins, Reverend Walker was asked to serve as Dr. Martin Luther King Jr.'s chief of staff. At a June 1, 1960 gathering in Petersburg, Dr. King assured citizens that Walker "is not leaving Petersburg but is going to a larger job to serve a better Petersburg."[338]

Existing Sites and Landmarks

The Site of the William R. McKenney Library
(Formerly Known as Petersburg Public Library)
137 South Sycamore Street, Petersburg, VA 23803

McKenney Library, the headquarters of the Petersburg Public Library System for many years, was originally a residence, built in 1859 by Petersburg Mayor John Dodson. After the Civil War, former Confederate General Billy Mahone lived there, and General Robert E. Lee stayed there as a guest. In 1923, then-owner Clara J. McKenney donated the house to the City of Petersburg for use as a library in honor of her late husband. The library operated in a segregated manner for decades, with separate floors for Black and white customers. In 1960, thanks to the efforts of activists, the library opened as an integrated facility—one of the first in Petersburg. In 2014, the library closed. The building is now in the process of being repurposed as a Black history museum.

PORTSMOUTH

Two Black dentists, Dr. Hugo A. Owens Sr. (1916–2008) and Dr. James W. Holley III (1926–2012), initiated the integration of Portsmouth Public Library, beginning with a letter-writing campaign in 1958. The library board resisted their appeals to desegregate the facility, taking no action on their request and canceling meetings when pressed to do so. When the board eventually agreed to study the matter in 1959, it announced that the library could integrate once it had a larger space, perhaps within two years (eyeing a post office building as the potential site of a larger library). Owens and Holley filed suit in federal district court, decrying the unfair treatment: "The conduct of discrimination by the Portsmouth Public Library based on race is humiliating, embarrassing and grossly unfair. This conduct tends to reasonably suggest and imply that your complainants and other Negroes are inferior."[339]

Compelled by the courts to respond, the library board lamented: "The present library quarters are so small, cramped and crowded as to make it impracticable to accommodate both races."[340] Another excuse was that Black and white teenagers might cause trouble with one another in an integrated library. To this, the judge replied, "I have a little bit more confidence in teenagers on these race problems than I do in adults."[341]

In 1960, a judge ruled that the Portsmouth library must be integrated. Linwood Williams, a sheet metal worker, was the first Black citizen to apply for and receive a library card at the newly desegregated Portsmouth library on March 1, 1960.[342] Holley went on to become the first Black mayor of Portsmouth, and Owens became the first Black rector at Old Dominion University.

Bertha Edwards and the Portsmouth Colored Community Library

Bertha Edwards worked in both segregated and integrated libraries during her thirty-five years of service with Portsmouth Public Library. *Esther Murdaugh Wilson Memorial Room, Portsmouth Public Library.*

Although it was ruled in 1960 that the main library must integrate, it wasn't until 1963 that the library moved into the remodeled post office with an integrated staff and library board. Until then, the Portsmouth Colored Community Library, which had served Black residents since 1945, remained in use. Bertha Winborne Edwards (1920–2009), a graduate of Hampton University, served as librarian at the nine-hundred-square-foot brick building for its entire existence, from 1945 to 1963.

The Portsmouth Colored Community Library traced its roots to the 1920s, when Black citizens, led by St. James Episcopal Church pastor M.B. Birchette, started a small community library that was housed in a few different locations until the addition of city funds allowed for a permanent building to be constructed and the collection to be expanded. But this library had nothing close to the resources of the white-only main library, and Owens deemed it "totally inadequate."[343]

Although the Portsmouth Public Library had a white-only policy prior to 1960, the Colored Community Library welcomed people of all races. White residents of nearby housing projects would sometimes use it, as would white travelers who were stopping to ask for directions. Edwards reported that she was always welcomed by librarians at Portsmouth Public Library, and the white librarian there sometimes ordered duplicate copies of reference books during segregation, giving one to Edwards for the "Colored" library. In return, Edwards shared the extensive collection of Portsmouth Black history documents she had amassed and preserved.[344]

Edwards was critical in building the Colored Community Library as a resource from its earliest days; she successfully argued to city officials that because Black people made up one-third of the population at the time, her library should receive one-third of the funding that was supplied to the white-only library. When she became part of the staff at the integrated Portsmouth Public Library in 1963, she was given the title of reference librarian. According to Dean Burgess, a retired director of the library, she ought to have been made director or assistant director. However, in 1960, when the State of Virginia began to require licenses for librarians, it retroactively conferred them on all staff currently serving as library directors—all except Edwards, apparently due to her race. This factor precluded her from obtaining the position of director or assistant director when the library integrated.[345] Edwards retired in 1980, having devoted thirty-five years of service to Portsmouth public libraries.

EXISTING SITES AND LANDMARKS

The Portsmouth Colored Community Library Museum
904 Elm Avenue, Portsmouth, VA 23704

The Portsmouth Colored Community Library served Black residents from 1945 to 1963. It was developed by members of the Black community, dating to the 1920s efforts of M.B. Birchette, the pastor of St. James Episcopal Church. The nine-hundred-square-foot, one-story brick building was originally located on South Street near Effingham Street. It has been moved twice and opened as a museum in 2013. The building is listed in the National Register of Historic Places.

Portsmouth Public Library
601 Court Street, Portsmouth, VA 23704

The original Portsmouth Public Library was established in 1914 in an annex behind the courthouse and was reserved for white residents only. It opened to people of all races in this building, a former post office, in 1963. Although the library had been legally compelled to integrate after a federal civil rights lawsuit in 1960, it wasn't until 1963 that the two smaller, formerly segregated libraries merged into this building with an integrated staff.

Top: The Portsmouth Colored Community Library operated from 1945 to 1963, overseen by librarian Bertha Edwards. It is now a Black history museum. *Authors' photograph.*

Middle: "Path of History" signage at Portsmouth Community Library, now a museum. *Authors' photograph.*

Bottom: Portsmouth Public Library opened in 1963 as an integrated facility with an integrated staff in this building, a former post office. *Authors' photograph.*

8

WASHINGTON, D.C.

*P*roximity to the District of Columbia (Washington, D.C.) was vital to many Black scholars and researchers in Northern Virginia, some of whom crossed the Potomac River to obtain opportunities they had been denied in Virginia. Samuel Tucker was among them. He attended Armstrong High School in Washington, D.C., as both high schools in Alexandria were for white students only. The only high school for Black students in Northern Virginia was Manassas Industrial School, which was much farther from Alexandria than Washington, D.C.

Tucker and his older brother George and younger brother Otto (later one of the library sit-in participants) commuted to the Washington, D.C. high school by streetcar. One June day in 1927, as the streetcar passed from Washington, D.C., into Virginia and became subject to Jim Crow laws, a white woman expected the boys to give up one of their seats. They refused. Upon reaching Alexandria, the boys were charged with disorderly conduct and abusive language. Fourteen-year-old Samuel was fined five dollars, and George was fined fifty cents, but an all-white jury later found the teenagers not guilty on appeal.[346]

After graduating from Armstrong High School and Howard University, Tucker used both the D.C. Public Library and the Library of Congress to study for the bar exam in the 1930s. Although these libraries were open to all users, regardless of race, they were not immune to discrimination.

The capital city suffered increased segregation following the election of President Woodrow Wilson. A Virginia native, Wilson had enticed Black

Americans to support his candidacy with promises of fairness. But after taking office in 1913, he endorsed the segregation of previously integrated federal offices, resulting in demotions and reduced pay for Black government employees.[347] Black staff in many federal workplaces found themselves relegated to segregated locker rooms, offices and dining areas. Black visitors to dining areas of federal buildings began to encounter segregated accommodations or even outright refusal of service. Both situations occurred to some extent at the Library of Congress.

THE LIBRARY OF CONGRESS

The Library of Congress (LOC), founded in 1800, is not known to have ever been segregated when it comes to accessing the collection or reading rooms. There were Black assistant librarians on staff in the mid-1800s, including bibliographer and historian Daniel Murray, whose career at the Library of Congress spanned fifty-one years, from 1871 to 1922. Murray was promoted to chief of periodicals when the Library of Congress moved into its own building in 1897. Dubbed "the father of Black bibliography," Murray's personal collection of pamphlets and books on Black social and political advancement is currently housed in the LOC's Rare Book and Special Collections and has been digitized.[348]

Postcard image, Library of Congress, Jefferson Building, Washington, D.C. Black Northern Virginian scholars, including Samuel Tucker, studied here. *Authors' collection.*

168

Murray was not the first or only Black staff member at the LOC in the nineteenth century. Frederick Fowler and Jon F.N. Wilkinson were both long-term Black employees whose careers overlapped Murray's tenure. Wilkinson began working in the Law Library in 1857 and was promoted to assistant librarian in 1872. Although his educational background was modest, he was so devoted to his work that he memorized much of the collection, making himself indispensable to researchers. Wilkinson worked in the library until the day of his death in 1912.[349] Fowler's career, in contrast, did not progress beyond routine tasks.

Murray had obtained a good education in Baltimore, despite his father having once been enslaved and his mother being illiterate. He began his Washington, D.C. career as a waiter in the Senate restaurant of the Capitol Building, where the Library of Congress was then located. There, he met the sixth Librarian of Congress, Ainsworth Rand Spofford, to whom he would eventually become a personal assistant.[350] This site of opportunity for Murray was to become the center of controversy decades later, as restaurants in federal buildings became increasingly segregated under Wilson's presidency.

On July 9, 1912, Congressman John H. Small of North Carolina wrote to the eighth Librarian of Congress, Herbert Putnam, complaining that "some ladies in whom I have an interest" were dining in the Library of Congress café when "a colored man and two colored women entered the room and were seated at the table nearest to them. I do not think this should be permitted."[351] Complaints such as this appear to have been handled by being deferred to dining service vendors on the issue of segregation.[352]

In this case, Putnam forwarded the complaint to the building and grounds superintendent, who replied to Small that while dining facilities in federal buildings were not typically segregated, "possibly some consideration is given to the proximity of seating at the table, and this, so far as feasible and practicable, I shall hereafter endeavor to accomplish." However, the superintendent added, due to the infrequency of Black visitors and limited space, it would not be possible to provide a separate room "for their convenience."[353]

While Murray was never required to deny service to Black customers while working in the Senate restaurant in 1870, worsening segregation after Wilson took office meant that visitors to restaurants in federal buildings became increasingly subject to discrimination. Members of the Washington, D.C. NAACP rose to combat this injustice.

In 1919, history teacher and Washington, D.C. NAACP officer Neval Thomas embarked in an effort to desegregate government dining facilities. Focusing on the D.C. Supreme Court, he began a letter-writing campaign that turned into a sit-in dubbed the "three-day siege," which resulted in desegregation of the court's dining facilities.[354] After this victory, Thomas turned his efforts toward segregation within the Library of Congress.

Thomas wrote U.S. House representative Norman J. Gould on October 28, 1919, deploring the "recent segregation of colored employees in the Library of Congress and the exclusion of the colored public from the public restaurant." He pointed out that this was a recent development:

> *These employees have worked there for over fifty years in perfect harmony, and the colored public have enjoyed this ordinary civil privilege for the same time without friction or injustice to anyone. A new superintendent of buildings and grounds there, who hails from the far south, now requires that colored employees eat separately behind a screen and that the colored public to* [sic] *be excluded from the public restaurant.*[355]

A June 9, 1922 letter finds Thomas still pursuing the issue. Writing to the new Superintendent of Buildings and Grounds Harriet Woods, he described Black customers being seated in a separate room with a "watchman whose sole duty is to keep colored patrons from entering the public restaurants."[356] He appealed to her to rectify the segregation instigated by her predecessor.

One of the incidents that garnered attention involved James Weldon Johnson, the Black former U.S. Minister to Nicaragua. Although he had dined in the Library of Congress café before without incident, one day, he arrived for lunch and was refused service. Senator James W. Wadsworth Jr., the chairman of the U.S. Senate Committee on Military Affairs, described the incident to café manager Catherine A. Leich in a letter dated January 20, 1920: "Mr. Seligmann and his colored friend, Mr. Johnson…went to the café at the usual lunch hour and asked to be served.…They were met by a man apparently in charge of the cafe, who, in a rough manner, told them they could not be served there.…The man in charge practically ordered them out." Having been told in a previous letter by Leich that she found no record of the event, he continued, "Their story is so circumstantial and they were so visibly upset that I find it impossible to believe that they made it up out of whole cloth."[357]

The incident was appealed all the way to President Wilson in a letter sent by Senator William M. Calder of New York, dated January 29, 1920. Referring to communication from NAACP secretary John R. Shillady, Calder wrote, "He complains that the colored race is discriminated against in the café of the Library of Congress…as the Library of Congress is under your jurisdiction, I [*sic*] submitting the matter to you for such action as you deem proper to take."[358] There is no record of a response from the president.

Shortly before Tucker used the Library of Congress to study for the bar exam, the situation was still not resolved. Oswald Garrison Villard, the editor of the *Nation* and a friend and one-time supporter of President Wilson, took up the cause. A white man, he was serving as vice-president of the integrated Washington, D.C. NAACP. He wrote to Putnam on January 2, 1929, decrying "deliberate and illegal discrimination" in the library's cafeteria. Putnam dismissed the charges as "general allegations," which he surmised were "a revival of one of some years ago, which we had supposed disposed of."[359]

To this, Dr. W.E.B. Dubois, a founder of the NAACP, shot back:

> *With regard to discrimination in the dining room of the Congressional Library…Mr. Herbert Putnam will find no difficulty at all in learning of discrimination against colored people. Sometimes they are refused outright, and sometimes they are seated back of screens or in a separate room. If he wishes a specific case, it would be easy to send a dozen persons to the library and prove my assertion.*[360]

Villard's next letter to Putnam raised the specter of legal action:

> *Mr. Putnam surely knows that the United States government cannot delegate to a concessionaire the right to break the law. Charles Sumner's civil rights law in full force in the District of Columbia and the Library of Congress has been the scene of the repeated breaking of this law.*[361]

During this flurry of letters, Superintendent of Buildings and Grounds W.C. Bond composed memorandums to several LOC departments, dated January 22, 1929, instructing staff to provide the same service to all customers, regardless of race. Bond was even more specific in his letter to Leich, dated the same day:

> *To ensure your understanding of our conversation the other day…no segregation or assignment of separate tables for colored people will be permitted and you should inform every one [sic] connected with the café and cafeteria that the same conveniences and attention must be given to all patrons, irrespective of their race or color.*[362]

Postcard image, interior, Library of Congress, Jefferson Building. Although the library was open to all races, some Black scholars reported being denied service in its dining areas. *Authors' collection.*

He then directed her to sign a copy of the letter to be kept on file. However, the incidents do not seem to have ended there. Current staff at the Library of Congress recall scholar John Hope Franklin, a recipient of the Presidential Medal of Freedom, "often noted in conversation with many of us that he was unable to use the eating facilities in the library." Franklin lived in the area as a professor at Howard University from 1947 to 1956.[363]

The ongoing dispute over discrimination in dining facilities is an example of how, even in integrated libraries, Black visitors risked inconvenience, insult and embarrassment. The potential for encountering such situations, even where they were as intermittent as they were at the Library of Congress, was another burden for Black scholars and researchers. The potential humiliation may well have dissuaded some from using the library altogether.

D.C. Public Library

The District of Columbia Public Library (DCPL) had a policy of integration since its 1903 opening. However, records indicate that some members of the library's board of trustees broached the idea of segregated branches in 1909.[364] While the segregation of DCPL branches never occurred, Neval Thomas once again stepped forward in the 1920s to call attention to inequities within the institution, as he had at the Library of Congress.

In 1922, Thompson wrote a series of letters to newspapers questioning why the D.C. Public Library's training class for white women, which had been active since 1905, excluded women of color. George F. Bowerman, DCPL's chief librarian from 1904 to 1940, had specifically declined to admit women of color to the training program in 1917. That year, he recommended establishing public libraries within "colored school buildings." But while he acknowledged that librarians of color would be needed to serve in them and that there was no training program for them other than at Howard University, he stated, "It would not be practicable to train such colored librarians in [DCPL's] own training class."[365]

In 1925, Thomas, who by then was the president of the Washington, D.C. chapter of the NAACP, continued to press for equity, publicly questioning why there were no Black librarians or staff members at DCPL. Bowerman replied that there were "colored" women on the janitorial staff.[366] DCPL did not have a Black librarian until Althea Howard joined the staff in 1943, three years after Bowerman's tenure ended.[367] Thomas did not live to see this milestone, as he passed away in 1930.

Howard University

Howard University in Washington, D.C., was also an essential resource for Black scholars in Virginia and elsewhere. Library desegregation activists Samuel Tucker, Dr. James W. Holley and W. Hale Thompson were graduates of Howard, and all moved back to their Virginia hometowns (Alexandria, Portsmouth and Newport News, respectively) after graduation to set up professional practices. Having had the advantages of Howard's Carnegie Library, which opened in 1910, as well as DCPL and the Library of Congress, it is even more understandable that they protested the injustice of inaccessible libraries near their Virginia homes. Neval Thomas, who advocated for equality within DCPL and LOC, was also a graduate of both Howard's undergraduate program and law school.

In appeals to Putnam to eliminate discrimination at the Library of Congress, Villard strongly recommended Putnam call on Mordecai Johnson, who became the first Black president of Howard University in 1926. Johnson, he wrote, "bids fair to be a great leader of his people; whose judgement has won the enthusiastic admiration of Theodore Roosevelt Jr. and many others."[368] He also name-dropped Howard University law professor Judge James Adlai Cobb, who later become the school's vice-dean. References to Howard University's leadership in these letters demonstrate the influence of the university and its faculty on civil rights issues.

Howard offered one of the only library education programs available to Black students in the early 1900s. Edward Christopher Williams held the titles "professor of bibliography, director of the library training class/Library School and librarian" from 1916 to 1929. He described the program in the course catalogue of 1916–17:

> *In response to the rather insistent, if somewhat limited, demand, particularly from the South, for opportunities for library training, and…to offer instruction in library science which shall meet the standards set by the American Library Association, the university will accept a limited number of students as members of a library training class.*[369]

The program's courses included reference work, bibliography, cataloguing, technical and administrative matters, as well as practical experience in the library. The library school was listed as a professional department within the university. However, as of 1916–17, it could accommodate only six incoming students. The curriculum was designed to be of practical use to those currently employed or soon to be employed in a library:

> *The work in its present form is designed primarily for persons already engaged in library work or fitting themselves for a definite position. The course, if followed earnestly, should fit the student for the management of a small school library or for intelligent work as assistant in a larger library.*[370]

Prior to Williams, Grace L. Hewett Watkins held the librarian/director of the Library School position from 1913 to 1916. Before that, Howard University offered a course in library economy taught by Flora L.P. Johnson as late as 1911–12. As one of the only library education programs available to Black students in the South, Howard's program likely shaped many segregated school and public libraries available to Black citizens during the Jim Crow era.

—————— Part III ——————

"A Deep-Seated Custom"

CONTEXT AND CONCLUSION

*Legally enforced segregation, however wrong it may be in principle, is nonetheless
a deep-seated custom in the South that cannot be quickly and rashly removed.*
—Harold Sugg

*People not only don't go where they aren't welcomed,
but people also many times don't go where they were used to being not welcomed.*
—Gene Ashton

CRITICAL OVERVIEW

Lack of Advocacy from Library Associations

Library professional associations were disappointingly passive when it came to the movement to desegregate public libraries. Despite advocacy from some individual white librarians in the South, notably Juliette Morgan of Montgomery, Alabama, and Ruth Brown of Bartlesville, Oklahoma, the American Library Association (ALA) did little to encourage the integration of southern libraries during the Jim Crow era. Although the ALA had passed its Library Bill of Rights in June 1939, just months prior to Samuel Tucker's sit-in at the Alexandria Library, the organization did not come to Tucker's defense.

Referring to 1946–64 attempts to dismantle Jim Crow practices, library historian Wayne Wiegand wrote: "At no time during these years did the American Library Association file any amicus brief in federal cases involving the desegregation of public libraries.…During these years, the association also allowed segregated libraries to hold full membership." It was not until 1960, after civil rights activists scored victories in Danville and Petersburg, Virginia, as well as elsewhere in the South, that the ALA began to address the issue.[371] Finally, in February 1961, the ALA adopted an addition to the Library Bill of Rights: "The rights of an individual to the use of a library should not be denied or abridged because of his race, religion, national origins or political views."

The Virginia Library Association (VLA) was similarly passive. During the VLA Annual Conference in Richmond on November 10–12, 1955, the "segregation controversy" was discussed in cautious terms by speaker Harold Sugg, associate editor of the *Norfolk Virginian-Pilot*. He opined that "legally enforced segregation, however wrong it may be in principle, is nonetheless a deep-seated custom in the South that cannot be quickly and rashly removed." He went on to warn of "damages that the extremes on both sides would cause." The write-up of the event in the official VLA publication, the *Virginia Librarian*, acquiesces to this "bothsidesism" framing of the issue.[372]

The acceptance of discrimination was belied by the appearance of progress in VLA literature of the time. The October 1955 issue of the *Virginia Librarian* advertises Black educator Saunders Redding as a dinner speaker at the upcoming VLA Annual Conference. Just under Redding's photograph is text inviting (presumably white) members to book a room at the luxurious Jefferson Hotel in Richmond, while "Negro members who plan to attend should correspond with Mrs. Verdelle Bradley, who will arrange for their accommodation at Virginia Union University."[373]

The lack of advocacy from library organizations during the Jim Crow era is especially disappointing considering the progress of 1925, when Hampton Library School was established. As part of Hampton Institute (now Hampton University) in Virginia, it enabled Black students to earn bachelor's degrees in library science and was one of only a few ALA-accredited library schools in the South.[374] Hampton graduate Thomas Fountain Blue launched the first Black library conference on March 15–18, 1927. It took place in the museum on campus and was attended by forty librarians from the South.[375] Sadly, the school closed in 1939, due to lack of sufficient funding. However, the college was able to retain some library science professors and courses after the degree program ended.

There were some cases of Black staff members being hired at white-only libraries prior to integration, as was the case with Frankie H. Jones at Danville Public Library in the 1930s and Gene Ashton at the Thomas Balch Library in Loudon County in the early 1960s. Ashton was known locally for his desegregation endeavors, particularly at the Tally-Ho Movie Theater. This could indicate that some white library staff did not agree with segregation and perhaps even sought to undermine it. Ashton's writings about his employment at Balch Library suggests the staff there did not agree with or enforce segregation.[376] However, it is also possible that Black staff were sometimes employed because they could be paid less than white staff.

Public Schools Versus Public Libraries

Public libraries typically become integrated prior to public schools. After *Brown v. Board of Education* (1954), the landmark U.S. Supreme Court decision that found racial segregation in public schools unconstitutional, segregationists became even more determined to fight school integration with all their might, engaging in the "Massive Resistance" movement.[377] While some segregationists fought the efforts to integrate public libraries for fear that it would open the gates for further integration, others thought it necessary to sacrifice library segregation to "save their strength" for the main battle over schools.[378] This sentiment can be traced through many newspaper editorials, articles and letters to the editors from the 1950s.

With *Brown II* (1955) the U.S. Supreme Court ordered that desegregation occur with "all deliberate speed"—a phrase vague enough to allow many states to stall the order.[379] The "Massive Resistance" policy was adopted in 1956 by the Virginia state government to block the desegregation of public schools. In 1959, the Virginia Supreme Court and a panel of federal judges separately ruled against "Massive Resistance" legislation, requiring the integration of public schools by those who had resisted *Brown v. Board*. Yet legal vestiges of resistance lingered throughout the 1960s and early 1970s.[380]

An editorial published in the *Blue Ridge Herald* and the *Richmond News Leader* in 1957 called "Silly Side of Segregation" opens with: "Virginia and the rest of the South would have a far better chance of maintaining racial separation in public schools if it were not for such foolish and irritating incidents as that reported from Purcellville in Loudoun County last week." After referencing Samuel Murray's inability to borrow a book and the ensuing legal action, the writer states: "This sort of thing, we are bound to say, is simply asinine. The Purcellville library serves the entire community....It is the only library there is. Negro citizens of course should have free and fair access to it." The writer continues, "Chance encounters of white and Negro in a public library, or on a bus or in a railway station or in an elevator, plainly do not involve relationships that are intimate, personal or prolonged. This impersonal sharing of public facilities constitutes no danger to public morals." The essay concludes, "It is sufficiently difficult to wage the fight as to schools, where racial separation can be justified; it will be impossible to win it if we seek to maintain segregation where segregation is silly."[381]

A June 13, 1960 editorial in the *Richmond Times-Dispatch* titled "Keep the Libraries Open!" voiced a similar sentiment, decrying public libraries that threatened to close rather than integrate, but it also put libraries in a separate category from other facilities. After expressing opposition to integration of schools, swimming pools, hotels and restaurants, the writer adds, "Libraries are in a different category. A library is a place where interracial contact is at a minimum and where students and readers sit quietly and mind their own business." The editorial reports that Virginia public libraries in Arlington, Charlottesville, Fairfax, Harrisonburg, Newport News, Norfolk, Portsmouth, Richmond, Roanoke and Winchester had integrated. "Do the people of Dansville and Petersburg wish to put themselves in a class apart and to abandon the well-nigh universal practice of making wisdom of the ages freely available to all?"[382]

As library historian Wayne Wiegand puts it: "Sometimes, public library integration was a sop to give the appearance of local progress on desegregating public accommodations, while whites continued to resist integration of institutions (like schools) they considered more important."[383] Just as many segregationists accepted integration of public libraries while opposing integration of schools, some prominent library donors who lobbied to keep libraries segregated raised funds to establish "colored libraries" in attempt to forestall integration under a cloak of magnanimity.[384]

Implicit Versus Explicit Segregation

In addition to formal segregation, where it is documented, there is evidence of implicit segregation of public libraries, even where Black residents were not specifically prohibited from using them. Oral interviews from those who were residents at the time indicate they do not remember seeing Black residents using public libraries that were in largely white neighborhoods.[385] Prior to the Fair Housing Act of 1968, housing discrimination and prejudicial treatment in granting zoning permits were rampant, reinforcing the segregation of neighborhoods.[386] Due to these barriers, along with transportation difficulties, access to libraries was often implicitly segregated by feasibility, even where it was not specified or enforced.

Library statistics, period accounts and oral histories indicate that Black residents often did not feel comfortable or welcome in libraries that were formerly white-only simply because the libraries had been compelled to integrate. The day after the formal integration of the Danville Public Library, seventy-eight white residents used the library; zero Black residents entered. Yet on that same day, twenty-five Black residents used the smaller "Colored" library that had been formerly available to them.[387] In Petersburg,

Virginia, there were also zero Black library users the first day the public library was formally open to people of all races. The Portsmouth Public Library reported that in the first month after desegregation, twenty-two Black customers applied for and received library cards; the following month, the number had risen to forty-seven.[388] In Loudoun County, a journalist reported that only one Black woman and her child had checked out books in the week following the desegregation of Purcellville Library.[389] Since all of these desegregation cases had been well publicized, it is unlikely that Black residents were unaware they had access to the libraries.

In his memoir, Danville native Evans Hopkins wrote of his vivid impression upon entering the newly integrated Danville Public Library as a child:

> *When the courts finally mandated that the library integrate, I was overjoyed. I remember arranging to ride into town with a teacher after school and rushing into the main library to the books that had been denied to me. But once inside the library, I discovered that all of the tables and chairs had been removed. In a final attempt to maintain segregation, city officials decided that while Blacks would have to be allowed into the library, they would not be permitted to sit and study alongside whites. When I recall the shock of seeing the spitefulness of whites evidenced by the bare floors of that library, I begin to understand how anger turns to rage.[390]*

Gene Ashton, who, as a Black high school student, had a job at the formerly segregated Thomas Balch Library in Leesburg, recounted seeing no other Black residents using the library during the time he worked there (1963 to 1964). He wrote, "People not only don't go where they aren't welcomed, but people also many times don't go where they were used to being not welcomed."[391]

A similar sentiment was voiced by Gertrude Evans, a Leesburg native who participated in demonstrations to desegregate Leesburg's Tally-Ho Movie Theater. During the events marking the anniversary of Purcellville Library's desegregation, she recalled, "When you know you're not wanted somewhere, you just don't feel comfortable [going in]. That's what segregation does."[392]

Conclusion

The history of the desegregation of public libraries in Northern Virginia—and Virginia as a whole—is more complicated than it may appear at first. Most public libraries were implicitly segregated at some time in their history, even though it was not explicitly stated. Early bookmobiles provided valuable service while library buildings were segregated, but many bookmobile services were also segregated. Typically, public libraries were desegregated before schools, but in some cases, school libraries extended valuable services to residents where public libraries were either absent or segregated.

Black citizens turned activists made the final push to desegregate libraries in Virginia that remained segregated into the 1950s and early 1960s. Their activism paved the way for more equitable library services and, in turn, expanded opportunities for their fellow citizens.

In Virginia and throughout North America, public libraries continue to evolve toward more inclusive practices. These practices include diversifying staff, eliminating fines and fees that inhibit use, deepening outreach to underserved communities and embracing principles of universal access. Knowledge of past injustices and the efforts involved in overcoming them empowers libraries to grow stronger in the future.

NOTES

Introduction

1. "Quintet Arrested for 'Library Sit-Down,'" *Washington Tribune*, August 26, 1939, 1.
2. Pew Research Center, "How Americans Value Public Libraries in Their Communities Summary of Findings," December 11, 2013, https://www.pewresearch.org/internet/2013/12/11/libraries-in-communities/.
3. This was a slight change from the 1942 Code of Virginia's wording regarding library services: "The service of books in county library systems receiving state aid shall be free and given to all parts of the county, region, city or town." The shift from requiring service be provided to "all persons" as opposed to locations made it clearer that, beginning in 1946 at least, library services must be extended to all individuals, regardless of race.
4. City officials often claimed segregated services were "equal" because residents had access to books from either library upon request. However, the card catalogues were typically in the whites-only libraries, making it difficult for Black residents to know what was available.

Chapter 1

5. Alexandria Library, "Alexandria Library Sit-In," https://alexlibraryva.org/1939-sit-in.
6. Minutes of the Alexandria Library Association, 1931–47, 150, 153, 158.
7. J. Douglas Smith, *Managing White Supremacy: Race, Politics, and Citizenship in Jim Crow Virginia* (Chapel Hill: University of North Carolina Press, 2002), 261–62.

8. Nancy Noyes Silcox, *Samuel Wilbert Tucker: The Story of a Civil Rights Trailblazer and the 1939 Alexandria Library Sit-In* (Fairfax, VA: History4All Inc., 2014), 41.

9. Smith, *Managing White Supremacy*, 260.

10. Ibid., 261.

11. Silcox, *Samuel Wilbert Tucker*, 45.

12. "Smash Va. Library Color Bar," *Baltimore Afro-American*, January 20, 1940.

13. Alexandria Library, "Sit-In."

14. Smith, *Managing White Supremacy*, 261.

15. Ibid., 262.

16. Alexandria Library Special Collection, "Letter from Samuel W. Tucker to Alexandria Library, February 13, 1940," https://alxndria.ent.sirsi.net/custom/web/lhsc/sitin/tuckerletter/doc.html.

17. *Out of Obscurity*, Documentary film, 2000, River Road Productions.

18. Boundary Stones, "Alexandria Sit-In, 1939," WETA's Local History, December 17, 2020, https://boundarystones.weta.org/2016/11/29/alexandria-library-sit-1939.

19. Brenda Mitchell-Powell, "The Robert H. Robinson Library," City of Alexandria, https://www.alexandriava.gov/historic/blackhistory/default.aspx?id=37350#TheSitDownStrikeandtheRobinsonLibrary.

20. Virginia Circuit Court for the City of Alexandria, October 18, 2019, docket MO19001660, https://media.alexandriava.gov/docs-archives/commattorney/info/librarysitinorder101819.pdf.

21. Library of Virginia, "Strong Men & Women in Virginia History," February 2022, https://edu.lva.virginia.gov/strong-men-women-in-virginia-history/.

Chapter 2

22. Jane Nida, transcript of an oral history interview, Center for Local History, Arlington Public Library, September 25, 1986.

23. Eleanor Lee Templeman, "Carrie M. Rohrer Memorial Library," in *Arlington Heritage: Vignettes of a Virginia County* (privately published: 1959), 190.

24. Arlington Public Library Center for Local History, "General Burdett and the Burdett Library," Arlington County Public Library Department Records, RG 29, https://libraryarchives.arlingtonva.us/Detail/objects/3310.

25. Arlington Public Library, "The Henry Louis Holmes Library, 1940-1949," February 17, 2022, https://library.arlingtonva.us/2022/02/17/the-henry-louis-holmes-library-1940-1949/.

26. Ibid.

27. Ibid.

28. Ibid.

29. Penrose Neighborhood Association, "History," http://penroseneighborhood.org/about-penrose/history/.

30. "Negro Librarians in Virginia Public Libraries Fall 1947," Records of the Public Library Development Division of the Virginia State Library and Archives,

1920–1992, accession 35467, State Government Records Collection, Library of Virginia, Richmond, VA, box 107, folder 7.

31. Judith Knudsen, manager of the Center for Local History of the Arlington Central Library, email to S. LaPierre, April 28, 2021.

32. Department of Community Planning, Housing and Development, "A Guide to the African American Heritage of Arlington County, Virginia," Historic Preservation Program, 55, 2016, https://discovery.apsva.us/wp-content/uploads/sites/14/2019/02/A-Guide-to-the-African-American-Heritage-of-Arlington-County-Virginia.pdf.

33. Arlington Public Library, "Henry Louis Holmes Library."

34. Arlington Public Library Center for Local History, "Dorothy M. Hamm Interview," 1986, https://libcat.arlingtonva.us/Record/28662.

35. Jane Nida, transcript of an oral history interview, Center for Local History, Arlington Public Library, September 25, 1986.

36. Judith Knudsen, manager of the Center for Local History, Arlington Central Library, email to S. Lapierre, April 28, 2021.

37. Ibid., Nida claims in this interview that "they [Black residents] were never excluded in the library system." However, her tenure began in the 1950s, after the system was formally integrated.

38. Personal communication with S. LaPierre, June 5, 2022.

39. Penrose Neighborhood Association, "History."

Chapter 3

40. Bernice Lloyd Bell, "Integration in Public Library Service in Thirteen Southern States, 1954–1962," PhD diss., Atlanta University, August 1963, 114.

41. "Plans Made for Founders' Day," *Manassas Journal*, June 10, 1943, 7.

42. "The Herndon Library," *Fairfax Herald*, June 29, 1900, 3.

43. Barbara Glakas, email message to Chris Barbuschak, May 12, 2021.

44. Ibid.

45. Connie P. Stuntz and Mayo S. Stuntz, *This Was Vienna, Virginia: Facts and Photos* (Vienna, VA, 1987), 239.

46. "Vienna Library Association, Incorporated," Fairfax County Charter Book 1, November 7, 1913, 314–16.

47. Fairfax County Board of Supervisors Minute Book 5, November 6, 1929, 506.

48. "County Library Plans Progressing," *Fairfax County Independent*, February 6, 1930, 1.

49. Ollie W. Tinner, *Fairfax County Colored Citizens Association Fairfax County, Va. Thirteenth Anniversary Achievement Number June 8, 1941* (Merrifield, VA, 1941), 3.

50. "County Library Rooms," *Fairfax Herald*, October 30, 1931, 1.

51. "To Be Opened," *Fairfax Herald*, July 22, 1932, 1.

52. "In New Location," *Fairfax Herald*, January 19, 1934, 6.

53. "County Library Moves," *Fairfax Herald*, January 11, 1935, 6.

54. "Library Moved," *Fairfax Herald*, March 4, 1938, 1.

55. "Fairfax Library Moves," *Fairfax Herald*, September 30, 1938, 1.
56. Fairfax County Board of Supervisors Minute Book 8, February 2, 1938, 29.
57. Fairfax County Deed Book F-6, July 30, 1900, 307.
58. "Fairfax Library," *Fairfax Herald*, June 23, 1939, 1.
59. "Constitution of the Fairfax Library Association, 1930," Fairfax County Public Library Records (unprocessed), MSS 10-01, Virginia Room, Fairfax County Public Library.
60. "Library Association Meets," *Fairfax Herald*, December 22, 1939, 6.
61. Fairfax County Board of Supervisors Minute Book 8, February 1, 1939, 299.
62. Ibid., March 15, 1939, 331.
63. Nan Netherton, *Books and Beyond: Fairfax County Public Library's First Fifty Years* (Fairfax, VA: Fairfax County Public Library, 1989), 1.
64. Fairfax County Public Library Board of Trustees Minutes, June 21, 1940.
65. "Bookmobile Will Arrive for Fairfax Next Tuesday," *Sun* (Arlington, VA), July 26, 1940, 1.
66. Fairfax County Board of Supervisors Minute Book 9, June 5, 1940, 135.
67. "Board of Trustees Fairfax County Free Library Summary of Statements," Fairfax County Public Library Records (unprocessed), MSS 10-01, Virginia Room, Fairfax County Public Library.
68. Fairfax County Public Library Board of Trustees Minutes, July 22, 1940.
69. Ibid., December 10, 1940.
70. Ibid., January 14, 1941.
71. "Monthly Report on Demonstration Area, Statewide Library Project, WPA, Virginia," January 1941, Fairfax County Public Library Records (unprocessed), MSS 10-01, Virginia Room, Fairfax County Public Library.
72. Fairfax County Public Library Board of Trustees Minutes, February 11, 1941.
73. Herbert Blunt, "Mobile Library Serves County," *Alexandria Gazette*, April 22, 1941.
74. Weekly Reports of Project Technicians and Assistant Project Technicians, 1941, Fairfax County Public Library Records (unprocessed), MSS 10-01, Virginia Room, Fairfax County Public Library.
75. Patricia Petrie, "The Fairfax County Public Library 1939–1962," (1962), 3.
76. *Statistics of Virginia Public Libraries* (Richmond: Extension Division, Virginia State Library, 1945).
77. *Statistics of Virginia Public Libraries* (Richmond: Extension Division, Virginia State Library, 1946).
78. Virginia General Assembly, "§ 42.1-55, Free Service Available to All, Code of Virginia, Chapter 3, State and Federal Aid," 2021, https://law.lis.virginia.gov/vacodefull/title42.1/chapter3/.
79. *Fairfax County Public Library* (Fairfax, VA, 1948); Records of the Public Library Development Division of the Virginia State Library and Archives, 1920–1992, accession 35467, State Government Records Collection, Library of Virginia, Richmond, VA, box 15, folder 3.
80. Letter, Ernestine Grafton to Margaret Edwards, June 1, 1945, Records of the Public Library Development Division of the Virginia State Library and Archives,

1920–1992, accession 35467, State Government Records Collection, Library of Virginia, Richmond, VA, box 15, folder 4.

81. Netherton, *Books and Beyond*, 3–4.

82. Jeff Clark, video producer of Fairfax County Public Schools, email message to Chris Barbuschak, June 11, 2021.

83. Tinner, *Fairfax County Colored Citizens Association*, 3.

84. "Colored School News," *Fairfax Herald*, December 20, 1940, 1.

85. Evelyn D. Russell-Porte, *A History of Education for Black Students in Fairfax County Prior to 1954* (Blacksburg: University Libraries, Virginia Polytechnic Institute and State University, 2000), 127.

86. Ibid., 207.

87. Fairfax County Public Library Board of Trustees Minutes, July 22, 1940.

88. Fairfax County School Board Minutes, August 20, 1940, https://insys.fcps.edu/schoolboardapps/ArchivedSBMinutes/1940-1949/19400820r.pdf.

89. Fairfax County School Board Minutes, October 1, 1940, https://insys.fcps.edu/schoolboardapps/ArchivedSBMinutes/1940-1949/19411001r.pdf.

90. Fairfax County School Board Minutes, March 16, 1943, https://insys.fcps.edu/schoolboardapps/ArchivedSBMinutes/1940-1949/19430315r.pdf.

91. Fairfax County Public Library, *Annual Report Fairfax County Public Library, Fiscal Year 1945–1946* (Fairfax, VA: Library Board of Trustees, 1946).

92. School reports, Fairfax County Public Library Records (unprocessed), MSS 10-01, Virginia Room, Fairfax County Public Library.

93. "Colored Library Opened in Vienna," *Fairfax Herald*, September 6, 1946, 1.

94. "Bailey's Cross Roads Negroes Get Library; More Books Sought," *Fairfax Standard*, [Summer] 1946.

95. Mary E. Elliott, *The Development of Library Service in Fairfax County, Virginia Since 1939* (Philadelphia: Drexel Institute of Technology, School of Library Service, 1951), 35.

96. Ibid, 49–54.

97. Jeff Clark, video producer, Fairfax County Public Schools, email message to Chris Barbuschak, June 11, 2021.

98. Memo, Wilbert T. Woodson to Robert F. Davis, July 6, 1959, W.T. Woodson Papers, MSS 06-03, Virginia Room, Fairfax County Public Library.

99. Fairfax County Public Library, *Fairfax County Public Library Annual Report 1963–1964* (Fairfax, VA: Library Board of Trustees, 1964), 2.

100. Fairfax County Board of Supervisors Minute Book 15, November 19, 1947, 385.

101. Netherton, *Books and Beyond*, 6.

102. Christine Coffey, *Report of a Survey of Certain Aspects of Public Library Service in Fairfax County* (Richmond: Virginia State Library, 1952), 1.

103. Ibid., 19.

104. Fairfax County Public Library Board of Trustees Minutes, May 15, 1952.

105. Fairfax County Public Library, *Fairfax County Public Library Annual Report, 1953–1954* (Fairfax, VA: Library Board of Trustees, 1954), 1.

106. Fairfax County Public Library Board of Trustees Minutes, August 17, 1953.

107. Friends of the Thomas Jefferson Library, "Libraries-Branches-Thomas Jefferson," vertical file, Virginia Room, Fairfax County Public Library.

108. Ibid.

109. "Library Reports Progress," *Fairfax County Sun Echo*, May 14, 1954, 1.

110. Netherton, *Books and Beyond*, 30.

111. Fairfax County Public Library Board of Trustees, *Statutory Basis, Functions, History, Present Service, Projected Service* (Fairfax, VA: Library Board of Trustees, 1955), 1.

112. FCPL Operating Budget Files, 1953–1958, Fairfax County Public Library Records (unprocessed), MSS 10-01, Virginia Room, Fairfax County Public Library.

113. Tom Burke, "Library Integration Suit Studied in Purcellville," *Sunday Star* (Washington, D.C.), February 24, 1957, A-13.

114. Bell, "Integration in Public Library Service," 114.

115. Maddy McCoy, email to Chris Barbuschak, June 12, 2021.

116. "Colored Library Opened," *Fairfax Herald*, 1.

117. "Vienna Library Notes," *Fairfax Herald*, June 14, 1946, 1.

118. Letter, June Waldrip to Ernestine Grafton, January 24, 1946; Records of the Public Library Development Division of the Virginia State Library and Archives, 1920–1992, accession 35467, State Government Records Collection, Library of Virginia, Richmond, VA, box 15, folder 5.

119. "Joyce Kilmer's Son Heads Vienna Unit," *Northern Virginia Sun*, February 13, 1959, 3.

120. "William Carter, Vienna Civic Leader," *Washington Post*, December 21, 1977, B-16.

121. Jennifer Lesinski, "Family Helps Change Face of Vienna," *Vienna Connection*, n.d.

122. Carol Bonham, "A Tale of Two Libraries," *Northern Virginian* 17, no. 5 (September/October 1987): 26–28.

123. Vienna Town Council Minutes, June 6, 1955, 5.

124. Letter, Kenton Kilmer to Florence Yoder, August 11, 1958; Records of the Public Library Development Division of the Virginia State Library and Archives, 1920–1992, accession 35467, State Government Records Collection, Library of Virginia, Richmond, VA, box 14, folder 11.

125. Fairfax County Public Library Board of Trustees Minutes, September 8, 1958.

126. Elsa Burrowes, email to Chris Barbuschak, May 8, 2021.

127. Beverly Schindler, "Vienna Apartment Zoning Approved," *Fairfax County Sun Echo*, October 23, 1958, 1.

128. Ibid.

129. Ibid.

130. Lynn C. Mitchell, "Vienna Library Asked to Desegregate," *Northern Virginia Sun*, October 16, 1958, 1.

131. Ibid.

132. *The Friends of the Library* (Vienna, VA: Friends of the Library, 1960); "Libraries-Branches-Patrick Henry," vertical file, Virginia Room, Fairfax County Public Library.

133. Beverly Schindler, "Vienna Library's Friends Organize," *Fairfax County Sun Echo*, February 19, 1959.

134. Barbara Scott, "Town-Based Library Dates to 1890s," *Vienna Times*, November 8, 1990, A1.

135. Fairfax County Public Library Board of Trustees Minutes, January 12, 1959.

136. Ross Netherton, *Annual Report of the Friends of the Library, Vienna, Virginia, January 27, 1970* (1970).

137. Fairfax County Public Library Board of Trustees Minutes, February 9, 1959.

138. Ibid., October 12, 1959.

139. Ibid., November 16, 1959.

140. Ibid., January 11, 1960.

141. Beverly Schindler, "Yeonas Donation of $2,500 Helps Vienna's Library," *Fairfax County Sun Echo*, September 8, 1960.

142. Beverly Schindler, "Vienna Council Defers Five-Year Plan," *Fairfax County Sun Echo*, October 6, 1960.

143. "Big Gift for Library," *Northern Virginia Sun*, September 9, 1960, B-1.

144. "Town Council Says 'OK' to Library Use," *Vienna Virginian*, January 25, 1962, 1.

145. Fairfax County Public Library Board of Trustees Minutes, December 19, 1960.

146. Ibid., March 13, 1961.

147. Ibid., January 8, 1962.

148. "Library Supporters," *Northern Virginia Sun*, April 3, 1962, 1.

149. Mary K. McCulloch, "New Headquarters for Fairfax Spars System-Wide Expansion," *Virginia Librarian* 9, no. 2 (Summer 1962): 16.

150. "First Day Busy at Branch," *Vienna Virginian*, April 12, 1962.

151. McCulloch, "New Headquarters," 16.

152. Ross Netherton, *Report of Activities of the Friends of the Library Vienna, Virginia, for 1968–1970* (1969), 3.

153. Scott, "Town-Based Library," A1.

154. Letter, Mary K. McCulloch to Florence B. Yoder, November 21, 1962; Records of the Public Library Development Division of the Virginia State Library and Archives, 1920–1992, accession 35467, State Government Records Collection, Library of Virginia, Richmond, VA, box 14, folder 10.

155. "Minstrel to Benefit Library," *Evening Star* (Washington, D.C.), November 23, 1956, B-2.

156. *Loudoun County African-American Historic Architectural Resources Survey* (Washington, D.C.: History Matters, LLC, 2004), 109.

157. Marriage certificate, Samuel Morgan to Dora Lee Johnson, May 24, 1980, Virginia Department of Health, Richmond, VA, Virginia Marriages, 1936–2014, roll: 101141829.

158. FCPL Operating Budget Files, 1959–1961, Fairfax County Public Library Records (unprocessed), MSS 10-01, Virginia Room, Fairfax County Public Library.

159. *Fairfax County Public Library Directory, July 1962* (Fairfax, VA: Fairfax County Public Library, 1962).

160. "Morgan, Dora Lee Johnson," *Washington Post*, February 26, 1999, B-7.

161. Fairfax County Public Library Board of Trustees Minutes, September 9, 1963.

162. Francis Barry, "A School Away from School in the Kingman Boys' Club," *Washington Post*, November 15, 1978, Z-1.

163. "Death Notice, Janice R. Bragg," *Washington Post*, May 27, 2020, B-7.

164. *Tiger* (Luther Jackson High School, 1959).

165. Mary K. McCulloch, interview, February 2, 1989, Northern Virginia Oral History Project collection, C0030, Special Collections Research Center, George Mason University Libraries.

166. Fairfax County Public Library Board of Trustees Minutes, September 19, 1973.

167. Abena Productions, "Darius Swann and Vera Swann," http://www.abenaproductions.com/vAUTHOR.HTM.

168. Harrison Smith, "Darius L. Swann, 95, Lead Plaintiff in Supreme Court Busing Case was Also Missionary in India," *Washington Post*, March 24, 2020, B-6.

169. *Policies of Fairfax County Public Library Board of Trustees Fairfax, Virginia* (Fairfax, VA: Fairfax County Public Library Board of Trustees, 1977), 8.

170. Fairfax County Public Library, "Patrick Henry Celebrates Black History Month," *Cross Reference*, March 1987, 1.

Chapter 4

171. "Falls Church Library," *Evening Star*, October 16, 1900, 12.

172. Melvin Lee Steadman, *Falls Church by Fence and Fireside* (Falls Church, VA: Falls Church Public Library, 1964), 154.

173. "Falls Church Library," *Evening Star*, 12.

174. *A Catalogue of Books* (Falls Church, VA: Library, 1903).

175. Steadman, *Falls Church*, 155.

176. Ibid.

177. Dorothy W. Birch, "A Brief History of 'Washington House,'" October 1972.

178. Lucina M. Bethune, "Semicentennial History of the Falls Church Library 1899–1950," in *Falls Church Public Library 1899–1961: A History* (Falls Church, VA: Library, 1961), 4.

179. "Falls Church to Have Gym Under New Plan," *Sun* (Arlington, VA), July 16, 1937, 1.

180. Hazel Adcock, "New Library's on Land of Woman Who Loved Books, Helped Town," *Northern Virginia Sun*, June 30, 1958, B-6.

181. Fairfax County Public Library Board of Trustees Minutes, July 22, 1940.

182. "F.C. Library Is Now on Free Basis," *Sun* (Arlington, VA), January 3, 1941, 1.

183. "Mrs. Mary Spencer New Librarian; Announces New Library Hours," *Sun Echo*, June 1946.

184. Jane B. Nida, "Progress Report of the Falls Church Library, February 1, 1953," in *Falls Church Public Library*, 24.

185. "Miss Drickamer Appointed Falls Church Librarian," *Evening Star*, October 13, 1949, B-1.

186. "'Better Reading' Awards Made," *Fairfax Standard*, May 26, 1950.

187. "War on Comic Books," *Washington Star Pictorial Magazine*, January 29, 1950, 12–13.

188. Beverly Bunch-Lyons, "Interview with Juanita Smith," 100 Years Black Falls Church, Virginia Tech Project, http://100yearsblackfallschurch.org/items/show/271.

189. "Wallace Costner Dies; Baptist Church Pastor," *Evening Star*, October 12, 1971, B-4.

190. Elsie Carper, "Pupils Leap Century in Moving into New Falls Church School," *Washington Post*, April 11, 1948, M18.

191. Fairfax County School Board Minutes, March 9, 1948, https://insys.fcps.edu/schoolboardapps/ArchivedSBMinutes/1940-1949/19480309s.pdf.

192. "Wallace Costner Dies," *Evening Star*, B-4.

193. "Edwin Henderson, Educator, 93, Dies," *Washington Post*, February 5, 1977, B6.

194. Frederic J. Frommer, "D.C. Introduced Anew to 'Father of Black Basketball,'" *Washington Post*, April 14, 2022, B1.

195. WMAL, interview with E.B. Henderson. Fairfax County Public Library.

196. Town Council Minute Book 1, January 11, 1915, 218–19.

197. Ibid., June 28, 1915, 231–33.

198. WMAL, interview with E.B. Henderson. Fairfax County Public Library, 13.

199. Falls Church Library Board Minutes, June 11, 1953.

200. "Author's Night Program Monday in Falls Church," *Fairfax Standard*, March 1950.

201. Christine Coffey, *Taking Stock of the Falls Church Public Library* (Richmond, VA: Virginia State Library, May 1950), 9.

202. "Falls Church Personals," *Sun* (Arlington, VA), September 29, 1950, 7.

203. Kay Martin Britto, telephone interview with Chris Barbuschak, April 28, 2022.

204. "Starting July 1: County Users of City Library Must Pay Fee," *Sun Echo*, February 12, 1954, 1.

205. Elizabeth M. Shaw, "A Data Sheet on Functional Services Written by the Librarian, Elizabeth M. Shaw, in Reply to a Request for Information for a Regional Fiscal Survey, 1955," *Falls Church Public Library*, 23.

206. Ibid., 27.

207. Falls Church Library Board of Trustees Minutes, September 28, 1955.

208. Ibid., November 10, 1955.

209. Ibid., December 7, 1955.

210. "Negro P-TA Warned on Complacency," *Washington Post*, November 12, 1955, 23.

211. Letter, Jean Strup to Dr. Edwin B. Henderson, December 8, 1955, Mary Riley Styles Library Archives.

212. "Policies and Procedures 1950–1959," Book Selection Policy of the Falls Church Public Library, September 13, 1956, Mary Riley Styles Public Library Archives.

213. Falls Church Public Library Manual of Library Policy and Procedures, April 10, 1957, Mary Riley Styles Public Library Archives.

214. Letter, Elizabeth M. Shaw to Reverend Wallace Costner, March 16, 1958, Mary Riley Styles Public Library Archives.

215. "Miss Stiles Named to Library Board," *Falls Church Echo*, October 17, 1952.

216. "Library Ground Broken," *Evening Star*, August 19, 1957, B-2.

217. "Falls Church Dedicates New City Hall, Library," *Washington Post*, July 5, 1958, A10.

218. "Dedication of Library, City Hall," *Fairfax Standard*, July 3, 1958.

219. E.B. Henderson, interview, 1962, Virginia Room, Fairfax County Public Library.

220. United States Information Service. "Evolution of a Typical U.S. Small City Library," *USIS Feature* nos. 59–270, 1959, 1.

221. "Como Funciona Una Tipica Biblioteca Pubica en Una Ciudad de los EE.UU," *LaEsfera*, November 18, 1959.

222. "Dedication of School Scheduled," *Northern Virginia Sun*, September 27, 1963, 20.

223. "M.E. Costner Leads First Class of Black Students Following Approval by Falls Church School Board," *Falls Church News-Press*, October 6, 2005, https://www.fcnp.com/2005/10/06/me-costner-leads-first-class-of-black-students-following-approval-by-falls-church-school-board/.

224. Richard Burns, "This Is the Fabric Itself," *Library Journal*, December 15, 1963, 4703.

225. Cora Slaughter, "A Library's First Book," *Washington Star Sunday Magazine*, December 6, 1964, 14.

226. "Spotlight on the Library," *Focus on Falls Church*, April 1965.

227. "Library Starts Oral Program," *Falls Church Globe*, May 14, 1965.

228. "A Day at the Library—Readers Coralled, Queried, Caught on Film by Reporter," *Falls Church Globe*, December 3, 1965, 17.

229. Jennifer Caroll, "Library Director Statement," City of Falls Church, June 2020, https://www.fallschurchva.gov/DocumentCenter/View/12678/LibraryDirector Statement_June2020.

230. Library Board of Trustees, "Statement from the Library Board of Trustees," City of Falls Church, 11, 2020, https://www.fallschurchva.gov/DocumentCenter/ View/12744/20200611-FINAL-Board-Statement-re-Social-Justice.

231. Mary Riley Styles Public Library, "FY 21 Annual Report July 1, 2020–June 30, 2021," 2021, https://www.fallschurchva.gov/DocumentCenter/View/5975/ Annual-Report.

232. "F.C. Library Goes Fine Free," *Falls Church News Press*, July 9, 2020, https://www.fcnp.com/2020/07/09/f-c-library-goes-fine-free/.

Chapter 5

233. Mrs. Murray's name is spelled "Josie Edith Cooke" on her marriage certificate. The Cook family name may be found with or without the "e" on historical documents.

234. Eugene Scheel, "Purcellville Library Became Public in 1957," *Loudoun Times Mirror*, March 18, 1962.

235. Ibid, 47.

236. "Library Denies Negro Book; Court Action Threatened," United Press, n.d., Thomas Balch Library Files.

237. Scheel, "Purcellville Library."

238. Ibid.

239. "Library Book Service Now Available to Everybody," *Blue Ridge Herald*, March 28, 1957.

240. Eugene Scheel, "Couple Wrote the First Chapter of County's Civil Rights Movement," *Washington Post*, April 8, 2001, J3.

241. Burke, "Library Integration Suit Studied," A-13.

242. "Library Bans Reporters from Meetings and Minutes," *Blue Ridge Herald*, May 2, 1957.

243. Scheel, "Couple Wrote."

244. Matthew Exline, *We Have Been Waiting Too Long: The Struggle Against Racial Segregation in Loudoun County, Virginia* (Ormond Beach, FL: Have History Will Travel Press, 2020), 56.

245. "Defenders Oppose Library Funds," *Loudoun Times-Mirror* (March 28, 1957).

246. Scheel, "Couple Wrote."

247. Email communication between M. Florer and S. LaPierre, June 10, 2021. Information about the Murrays creating décor for the Eisenhower home came from historian Eugene Scheel's 2001 interview with Josie Murray (verified via an email communication between E. Scheel and S. LaPierre, June 21, 2021). According to Michael R. Florer, MA, a museum curator and library manager at Eisenhower National Historic Site, "The Eisenhowers hired an interior designer for their Gettysburg home. Her business was Elisabeth Draper Inc. and located in New York City. Though she did all the designing, she contracted out some and perhaps most of the production of various furnishings. So, there is the possibility of the Murrays doing work for the Eisenhowers through Elisabeth Draper."

248. "Library Was Ordered 10 Years Ago to Serve All, Regardless of Race," *Blue Ridge Herald*, February 28, 1957.

249. Letters in the files of Thomas Balch Library.

250. Meredith Thomas and the Purcellville Preservation Association, *Purcellville: Images of America* (Charleston, SC: Arcadia Publishing, 2011), 33.

251. Gene Ashton changed his name to Cooper-Moore.

252. Gene Ashton, personal account from the vertical file "African American History—Integration of Thomas Balch Library," collection of Thomas Balch Library.

253. Exline, *We Have Been Waiting*, 86–94.

254. Jim Barnes, "The Tales of the Two Loudouns: Library Program to Mark the End of Segregation in the County 60 Years Ago," *Washington Post Loudoun Extra*, April 2, 2017.

255. Loudon 100, "Reginald 'Reggie' Simms," https://www.loudoun100.com/video-series/reggie-simms.

256. Scheel, "Purcellville Library."

257. Joseph Cook's son Leslie, also known as Junius, fathered Josie.

258. Friends of the Thomas Balch Library, *The Essence of a People II* (Leesburg, VA: Black History Committee of the Friends of the Thomas Balch Library, 2002), 49.

259. Barnes, "Tales of the Two Loudouns."

260. Carver Alumni Association. https://www.carveralumni.com/.

261. Friends of the Thomas Balch Library, *The Essence of a People* (Leesburg, VA: Black History Committee of the Friends of the Thomas Balch Library, 2004), 19–20.

262. Asa Moore Janney and Werner L. Janney, eds., *John Jay Janney's Virginia: An American Farm Lad's Life in the Early 19th Century* (EPM Publications Inc., 1978), 56.

263. Scheel, "Purcellville Library."

264. Congressional Record, "Extensions of Remarks," April 12, 2017, E501, https://www.congress.gov/115/crec/2017/04/12/CREC-2017-04-12-pt1-PgE500-4.pdf.

Chapter 6

265. Advertisement, *Manassas Journal*, January 26, 1933, 2.

266. E.H. Rion, "Catharpin," *Manassas Journal*, November 3, 1949, 3.

267. Donald E. Curtis, *The Curtis Collection: A Personal View of Prince William County History* (Prince William, VA: Prince William County Historical Commission, 1988), 154.

268. Lucy W. Phinney, *Yesterday's Schools: Public Elementary Education in Prince William County, Virginia, 1869–1969, A Social and Educational History of a Rural County in Virginia* (1993), 26.

269. David Nasaw, *Andrew Carnegie* (New York: Penguin Books, 2007), 607.

270. Andrew Carnegie, "The Best Fields for Philanthropy," *North American Review* 149, no. 397 (December 1889): 690–91.

271. "Origin of Local School Library," *Manassas Journal*, September 10, 1942, 1.

272. "Silver Tea for Library," *Manassas Journal*, November 3, 1927, 4.

273. "Robert E. Lee Exhibit of the Ruffner-Carnegie Library," *Manassas Journal*, January 14, 1937, 1.

274. "Library Notice," *Manassas Journal*, June 11, 1936, 1.

275. Clarence Wagener, "Eugenia Hilleary Osbourn, Her Life, Work and Influence," *Manassas Journal*, May 3, 1951, 4.

276. "Alumni Assist Library Move," *Manassas Journal*, June 9, 1938, 1.

277. "Formal Opening of Library," *Manassas Journal*, March 10, 1938, 1.

278. Prince William Public Library System Scrapbook, vol. 1, 1952–1967, Ruth E. Lloyd Information Center (RELIC), Central Library, Manassas, VA.

279. "For Colored Youth," *Sunday Star*, February 11, 1906, 10.

280. Laura Ann Peake, "The Manassas Industrial School for Colored Youth, 1894–1916," PhD diss., College of William & Mary, 1995, 77.

281. Ibid., 29–30.

282. Frederick Douglass, "Frederick Douglass Papers: Speech, Article, and Book File, 1846–1894; Speeches and Articles by Douglass, 1846–1894; Sept. 3, 1894, Speech at the Dedication of the Manassas Industrial School, Manassas, Va., Typescript and Clippings," manuscript/mixed material, retrieved from the Library of Congress, www.loc.gov/item/mss1187900491/.

283. "For Colored Youth," *Sunday Star*, 10.

284. Peake, "Manassas Industrial School for Colored Youth," 72.

285. "Mr. Villard Accepts," *Evening Star*, January 19, 1905, 9.

286. Manassas Industrial School for Colored Youth, *1915–16 Catalog* (Manassas, VA: Manassas Industrial School for Colored Youth, 1915).

287. Thomas J. Jones, *Negro Education: A Study of the Private and Higher Schools for Colored People in the United States*, vol. 1 (Washington, D.C.: Department of the Interior, Bureau of Education, 1917), 173.

288. Thomas J. Jones, *Negro Education: A Study of the Private and Higher Schools for Colored People in the United States*, vol. 2 (Washington, D.C.: Department of the Interior, Bureau of Education, 1917), 610.

289. Morgan Breeden, *Minutes of the Prince William County School Board July 7, 1943–June 16, 1947, Book 6* (2014), 67.

290. Ibid., 94.

291. Eugene M. Scheel, *Crossroads and Corners: A Tour of the Villages, Towns and Post Offices of Prince William County, Virginia Past and Present* (Prince William, VA: Historic Prince William Inc., 1996), 48.

292. Sarah M.D. Turner, *Haymarket: A Town in Transition: Highlights of the History of the Town* (Haymarket, VA: Prepared by the Haymarket Historical Commission, 1998), 141.

293. "Haymarket Library Opens," *Manassas Journal*, August 5, 1921, 1.

294. "Library Temporarily Closed," *Manassas Journal*, January 19, 1923, 1.

295. "The Woman's Club of Haymarket," *Manassas Journal*, June 11, 1931, 6.

296. "A Brave Little Library," *Manassas Messenger*, July 18, 1947, 10.

297. "Miss Eugenia Osbourn Honored by Woman's Club," *Journal Messenger*, July 17, 1952.

298. "Women's Club Meets Monday at Trinity," *Manassas Journal*, October 18, 1951, 7.

299. "Eugenia Osbourn Honored," *Journal Messenger*.

300. Fairfax County Public Library Board of Trustees Minutes, February 11, 1952.

301. "Eugenia Osbourn Honored," *Journal Messenger*.

302. Ibid.

303. Prince William Public Library System Scrapbook, vol. 1, 1952–1967, Ruth E. Lloyd Information Center (RELIC), Central Library, Manassas, VA.

304. Prince William Public Library Board of Trustees Minutes, May 29, 1952.

305. Prince William Public Library System Scrapbook, vol. 1, 1952–1967, Ruth E. Lloyd Information Center (RELIC), Central Library, Manassas, VA.

306. Ibid.

307. Donald L. Wilson, Virginiana librarian, Ruth E. Lloyd Information Center for Genealogy and Local History (RELIC), Prince William Public Libraries, email to S. LaPierre, May 4, 2021.

308. Prince William Public Library System Scrapbook, vol. 1, 1952–1967, Ruth E. Lloyd Information Center (RELIC), Central Library, Manassas, VA.

309. Ibid.

310. Prince William Historic Preservation Division, "7th Annual Prince William/Manassas History Symposium: The Courageous Four," YouTube, April 18, 2022, https://www.youtube.com/watch?v=ISw05D84vmI.

311. Ibid.

312. Prince William Public Library Board of Trustees Minutes, December 8, 1953.

313. "Art Exhibit on Display at Library," *Journal Messenger*, May 7, 1953.

314. Aaron Betz phone interview with Chris Barbuschak, May 9, 2022.

315. Prince William Public Library System Scrapbook, vol. 1, 1952–1967, Ruth E. Lloyd Information Center (RELIC), Central Library, Manassas, VA.

316. "New County Library Opens," *Journal Messenger*, September 20, 1962, C-1.

317. "Books on Civil War Era Loaned to County Library," *Journal Messenger*, August 1964.

318. Prince William Public Library Board of Trustees Minutes, December 27, 1965.

319. "New County Structure Will Open," *Evening Star*, September 15, 1965, D-24.

320. Prince William Public Libraries, "Library Locations & Hours," https://www.pwcva.gov/department/library/branch-locations-hours.

321. Jill Palermo, "'Lifting People Up': Manassas Officials Unveil Long-Awaited Jennie Dean Statue," *Prince William Times*, October 24, 2020, https://www.princewilliamtimes.com/news/lifting-people-up-manassas-officials-unveil-long-awaited-jennie-dean-statue/article_587756fc-162f-11eb-b724-4b8f073d801a.html.

322. Cari Shane, "5,193 Public Sculptures. 4,799 Are Men. 394 Are Women," *Washington Post*, April 17, 2011, E1.

323. Phinney, *Yesterday's Schools*, 142.

Chapter 7

324. Eliza Atkins Gleason, *The Southern Negro and the Public Library: A Study of the Government and Administration of Public Library Service to Negroes in the South* (Chicago: University of Chicago Press, 1941), 90.

325. Ibid, 92.

326. Wayne A. Wiegand and Shirley A. Wiegand, *The Desegregation of Public Libraries in the Jim Crow South: Civil Rights and Local Activism* (Baton Rouge: Louisiana State University Press, 2018), 91.

327. In his memoir, *Life After Life*, writer Evans Hopkins relates his experience as a child using the tiny two-room library that was reserved for Black residents of Danville; it held "books discarded from the segregated main library" but was nevertheless a place of discovery for the avid reader.

328. Evans D. Hopkins, *Life After Life: A Story of Rage and Redemption* (New York: Free Press, 2005), 98.

329. Hattie Thomas Lucas, *Huntington High School: Symbol of Community Hope and Unity* (Yorktown, VA: Publishing Connections, 1999), 64.

330. Pat Taylor, personal conversation with S. LaPierre, August 22, 2021.

331. Carl Tobias, "Untenable, Unchristian, and Unconstitutional," University of Richmond School of Law Scholarship Repository, 58 Mo. L. Rev. 855, 1993.

332. "Library Desegregation Asked by Kin of Donor," *Washington Post-Times-Herald*, April 5, 1960.

333. Markus Schmidt, "The 50ᵗʰ Anniversary of the Petersburg Library Sit-in, the First of the Civil Rights Era," Progress-Index, February 26, 2010, https://www.progress-index.com/story/news/2010/02/26/the-50th-anniversary-petersburg-library/33203475007/.

334. Wiegand, *Desegregation of Public Libraries*, 84.

335. Tobias, "Untenable, Unchristian, and Unconstitutional."

336. Walker and her four children were home alone two weeks later when someone threw a bottle containing an obscene note signed "KKK" at their window. The next day, the family requested and received police protection. Theresa Walker later became one of the Freedom Riders. She still lives in Virginia.

337. "Sit-Ins Lead to Arrests; Those Jailed Called 'Only Free People' in Petersburg," *Progress-Index*, February 26, 2010, https://www.progress-index.com/story/news/2010/02/27/sit-ins-lead-to-arrests/36482234007/.

338. "Negro Leader Urges Continued Struggle," *Richmond News Leader*, June 2, 1960.

339. Wiegand, *Desegregation of Public Libraries*, 61.

340. Ibid.

341. Ibid.

342. "Portsmouth Library Open," *Norfolk New Journal and Guide*, March 12, 1960.

343. Wiegand, *Desegregation of Public Libraries*, 60.

344. PCTV Channel 48, "Remarkable Portsmouth: Episode 1, Bertha Winborne Edwards," YouTube, January 6, 2020, https://www.youtube.com/watch?v=ZSbnFEU7LIs.

345. Ibid.

Chapter 8

346. Smith, *Managing White Supremacy*, 260–61.

347. Abhay Aneja and Guo Xu, "The Costs of Employment Segregation: Evidence from the Federal Government under Wilson," *IRLE Working Paper*, no. 108–20 (2020), http://irle.berkeley.edu/files/2020/12/The-Costs-of-Employment-Segregation.pdf.

348. John Y. Cole, "Daniel Murray: A Collector's Legacy," Library of Congress, https://www.loc.gov/collections/african-american-perspectives-rare-books/articles-and-essays/daniel-murray-a-collectors-legacy/.

349. Elizabeth Dowling Taylor, *The Original Black Elite: Daniel Murray and the Story of a Forgotten Era* (New York: HarperCollins, 2017), 27.

350. Ibid.

351. Manuscript Division, Records of the Library of Congress, Central File, Macleish-Evans, box 694, Cafeteria 1902–1939 (B&G 2-5-1).

352. Cheryl Fox, Library of Congress Archives and library history specialist, personal communication with S. LaPierre, March 24, 2022.

353. Manuscript division, Records of the Library of Congress, Central File, Macleish-Evans, box 694, Cafeteria 1902–1939 (B&G 2-5-1).

354. Derek Gray, *The NAACP in Washington, D.C.: From Jim Crow to Home Rule* (Charleston, SC: The History Press, 2022), 85–86.

355. Frank Lloyd Averill was the superintendent of buildings and grounds at that time, having been appointed by the president in 1915.

356. Manuscript division, Records of the Library of Congress, Central File, Macleish-Evans, box 694, Cafeteria 1902–1939 (B&G 2-5-1).

357. Ibid.

358. Ibid.

359. Ibid.

360. Ibid.

361. Ibid.

362. Ibid.

363. SEM, reference librarian, Library of Congress, personal communication with S. LaPierre, March 24, 2022.

364. Derek Gray, DCPL archivist, personal communication with S. LaPierre, March 25, 2022.

365. Gray, *NAACP in Washington*, 104.

366. "Makes Personal Visit to Librarian," *Washington Eagle*, November 4, 1922.

367. Gray, *NAACP in Washington*, 104.

368. Manuscript division, Records of the Library of Congress, Central File, Macleish-Evans, box 694, Cafeteria 1902–1939 (B&G 2-5-1).

369. Howard University, "Catalogue of the Officers and Students of Howard University, 1916–17," 143–44, https://dh.howard.edu/cgi/viewcontent.cgi?article=1048&context=hucatalogs.

370. Ibid.

Chapter 9

371. Susan Lee Scott, "Integration of Public Library Facilities in the South: Attitudes and Actions of the Library Profession," *Southeastern Librarian* 18 (Fall 1968): 162.

372. "1955 Conference A Success," *Virginia Librarian* 2, no. 4 (January 1956): 37–38.

373. "VLA Conference Meets at Richmond November 10–12," *Virginia Librarian* 2, no. 3 (October 1955): 26.

374. S.L. Smith, "The Passing of the Hampton Library School," *Journal of Negro Education* 9, no. 1 (1940): 51–58.

375. The Hampton Library School was founded with a grant from Carnegie Corporation in 1925. The Carnegie Corporation also funded the 1927 conference.

376. Gene Ashton, personal account, vertical file, Thomas Balch Library.

377. Smith, *Managing White Supremacy*, 8–9.

378. Exline, *We Have Been Waiting*, 57.

379. National Archives, "Educator Resources," August 15, 2016, https://www.archives.gov/education/lessons/brown-v-board/timeline.html.

380. James Hershman, "Massive Resistance," Encyclopedia Virginia, December 7, 2020, https://encyclopediavirginia.org/entries/massive-resistance.

381. "Silly Side of Segregation," *Blue Ridge Herald*, reprinted from the *Richmond News Leader*, February 28, 1957.

382. "Keep the Libraries Open!" *Richmond Times-Dispatch*, June 13, 1960.

383. Wayne A. Wiegand, *Part of Our Lives: A People's History of the American Public Library* (New York: Oxford University Press, 2015), 173.

384. Exline, *We Have Been Waiting*, 56.

385. Ibid.

386. Everard Munsey, "Hardships of Negroes in Fairfax Deplored," *Washington Post*, November 29, 1961, C1.

387. Wiegand, *Desegregation of Public Libraries*, 98.

388. Helen Kirkpatrick, "Portsmouth Public Library," *Virginia Librarian* 7, no. 2 (Summer 1960): 30.

389. "Defenders Oppose Library Funds," *Loudoun Times Mirror*, March 28, 1957.

390. Hopkins, *Life After Life*, 14–15.

391. Gene Ashton, personal account, vertical file, Thomas Balch Library.

392. Barnes, "Tales of the Two Loudouns."

INDEX

ABOUT THE AUTHORS

Chris Barbuschak, a Fairfax County native with a passion for local history, is an archivist/librarian in Fairfax County Public Library's Virginia Room. He gets paid to do what he loves: making Northern Virginia historical records and photographs publicly accessible and assisting researchers with their historical and genealogical quests. A graduate in history from Loyola University Chicago, he received his MLIS from Dominican University. He previously worked for the *Chicago Tribune* as a photograph archivist and for the Chicago Public Library system. Outside of the library, he can be found road-tripping across the country, always in search of the next best vintage diner to experience.

Suzanne S. LaPierre is a Virginiana specialist librarian for Fairfax County Public Library in Virginia. Her writing has been published in national and international journals, including *Public Library Quarterly* and *Computers in Libraries*. She authors "The Wired Library" column for *Public Libraries Magazine* and is a contributing writer for the 2022 edition of *Library and Book Trade Almanac*. In addition to holding a MLIS from the University of South Carolina, she has an MA in Museum Studies from the George Washington University and a BFA from Rhode Island School of Design. Along with her coauthor, she was awarded the 2022 Heritage Preservation Award from Historic Vienna Inc. for the research that resulted in this book.

3/23

Visit us at
www.historypress.com